Super interesting
facts for smart kids

1000 amazing facts for curious minds about science, history, animals, and other awesome things.

Contents

SPACE

THE UNIVERSE

- o The universe is unimaginably huge, containing everything that exists, from galaxies and stars to planets and even tiny particles. Our solar system is just a speck within this vast cosmos.

- o A galaxy is a vast collection of stars, planets, gas, and dust held together by gravity. Our home galaxy is called the Milky Way, and it's estimated to contain over 100 billion stars!

- o The universe is constantly expanding. Galaxies are moving away from each other, and this discovery led scientists to theorize that the universe began with a colossal explosion called the Big Bang.

  The universe is about 13.8 billion years old. That's an incredibly long time, but it's only a small fraction of the universe's potential lifespan.

- o Galaxies often interact with each other due to gravity, sometimes resulting in beautiful collisions and mergers. These events can trigger the formation of new stars and even reshape the galaxies' structures.

- o The visible universe—including Earth, the sun, other stars, and galaxies—is made of protons, neutrons, and electrons bundled together into atoms. Perhaps one of the most surprising discoveries of the 20th century was that normal matter makes up less than 5 percent of the mass of the universe. The rest of the universe appears to be made of a mysterious, invisible substance called dark matter (25 percent) and a force that repels gravity known as dark energy (70 percent).

- o The speed of light is super-fast! It can travel around the Earth seven times in just one second.

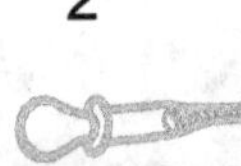

- Black holes are incredibly dense objects with gravity so strong that nothing, not even light, can escape their grasp. They form when massive stars collapse under their weight.

- Some galaxies "eat" smaller galaxies through a process called galactic cannibalism. Over time, more giant galaxies grow by absorbing smaller ones.

- Some theories suggest that our universe might be just one of many universes in a larger "multiverse." Each universe could have its own set of physical laws and properties.

- In 2015, scientists detected gravitational waves—ripples in space-time caused by powerful cosmic events, like colliding black holes. This discovery opened up a new way of observing the universe.

- Despite our progress in understanding the universe, there are still many mysteries to unravel. Questions about dark matter, dark energy, and the nature of space-time continue to challenge scientists and fuel our curiosity.

- A nebula is a giant cloud of dust and gas in space. Some nebulae come from the gas and dust thrown out by the explosion of a dying star, such as a supernova. Gravity can slowly begin to pull together clumps of dust and gas and as these clumps get bigger and bigger, their gravity gets stronger and stronger.
Eventually, the clump of dust and gas gets so big that it collapses from its own gravity. The collapse causes the material at the center of the cloud to heat up-and this hot core is the beginning of a star.

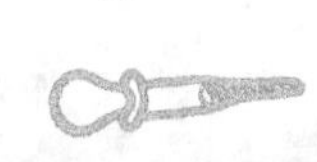

- o   The Hubble Space Telescope, like a super powerful camera in space, can see galaxies that are billions of light-years away.

- o   If you go outside on a clear night, you can see the International Space Station (ISS) pass by as a bright dot moving across the sky.

- o   Gaze into the night sky, and you might spot our cosmic neighbor, the Andromeda Galaxy. Although it's our closest galactic friend, its light takes over 2 million years to reach us, a testament to the vastness of space.

- o   In April 2019, scientists captured the first-ever image of a black hole using a network of telescopes around the world. This breakthrough provides new insights into these mysterious cosmic objects.

- o   Space is a very cold place at –270.45 Celsius! Luckily space suits are very well insulated to keep the astronauts warm in the cold conditions.
  They absorb body heat and then when the body needs warmth, it will release heat. Clever!

- o   The question of whether space is infinite is still a topic of scientific exploration. While space appears to be vast and limitless, our current understanding suggests that the observable universe, which includes all the matter and energy we can detect, is finite but continuously expanding. However, beyond the observable universe, it remains uncertain whether space is truly infinite or has boundaries that are yet to be discovered. Scientists continue to study and theorize about the nature of space.

- o   A spoonful of a neutron star would weigh about 6 billion tons on Earth. Neutron stars are incredibly dense!

THE SUN

- If Earth were to snuggle as close to the Sun as Mercury does, we'd find ourselves in a searing embrace. The Sun's fiery rays would scorch the landscape, a reminder of the importance of our perfect distance.

- The Sun isn't just a glowing ball; it's a space weather factory! It constantly sends out a stream of particles called solar wind. When this wind meets Earth's magnetic field, it creates dazzling auroras - nature's very own light show.

- The sun is about 10,000 degrees Fahrenheit.

- Standing on Mercury's surface, the Sun would loom nearly three times larger in the sky compared to Earth. This solar spectacle is a consequence of Mercury's proximity to our fiery star.

- The Sun, a cosmic behemoth, is so colossal that it could envelop more than a million Earths within its immense sphere. This fiery giant commands its domain, radiating life-giving energy across the solar system.

- The Solar System formed about 4.6 billion years ago.

- Throughout history, various cultures and civilizations have worshiped and revered the Sun as a powerful deity. Its life-giving properties have inspired countless myths, rituals, and celebrations.

- In the Sun's core, temperatures and pressures are incredibly high. Hydrogen atoms collide with each other so forcefully that they fuse, creating helium and releasing energy. This process is similar to what happens in hydrogen bombs but on a much larger and more controlled scale.

o Light-Speed Journey: It takes about 8 minutes and 20 seconds for sunlight to travel from the Sun to Earth. So when you look at the Sun, you're seeing it as it was over 8 minutes ago!

o Sunspots are temporary dark areas on the Sun's surface caused by its magnetic activity. These spots can be bigger than Earth and can impact the Sun's brightness and temperature.

o During a solar eclipse, the Moon aligns perfectly between the Earth and the Sun, temporarily blocking out its light. This rare event creates a fascinating display in the sky, turning day into twilight.

o The Sun is about 4.6 billion years old and is middle-aged. It has been shining for billions of years and will continue to do so for several billion more. Eventually, it will exhaust its hydrogen fuel and expand into a red giant before shedding its outer layers and becoming a white dwarf.

o Despite being the center of our solar system, the sun never stays in one place. It's continuously orbiting around the Milky Way galaxy at a speed of around 503,311 miles per hour. The galaxy is so huge, though, that it still takes the sun about 226 million years to move through it one time!

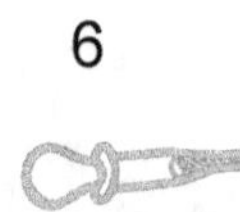

THE STARS

- A star is a massive, bright, sphere of very hot gas called plasma which is held together by its gravity.

- Stars radiate energy created from nuclear fusion, which is a process that takes place in a star's core and involves hydrogen fusing (burning) to make helium.

- As a star nears the end of its life, it begins to change helium into heavier chemical elements, such as carbon and oxygen, and the star will begin to change color, density, mass, and size.

- After the Sun in our Solar System, the nearest star to Earth is Proxima Centauri. It is about 39.9 trillion km away or 4.2 light years. This means it takes light from this star 4.2 years to reach Earth. Using the newest, fastest space probe propulsion systems would still take a craft about 75,000 years to get there.

- There are approximately 200-400 billion stars in our Milky Way Galaxy alone.

- Each galaxy contains hundreds of billions of stars and there are estimated to be over 100 billion galaxies in the universe. So the total number of stars in the universe is mind-boggling, estimated to be at least 70 sextillions and possibly as high,as 300 sextillions, that's 300,000,000,000,000,000,000,000!!!!!

- Binary stars and multi-star systems are two or more stars that are gravitationally linked, they orbit around each other.

Most stars are much older than the sun. Stars are usually between 1 and 10 billion years old. Some stars may even be close to the age of the observed universe at nearly 13.8 billion years old. Scientists can determine the age of a star by studyingits brightness, temperature, and other characteristics.

- The most common stars are red dwarfs. They are less than half the size and mass of our Sun and burn their fuel very slowly so live longer than any other type of star, over 100 billion years. Red dwarfs are cooler in temperature than most stars and so shine less, eventually getting dimmer, they do not explode.

- A brown dwarf forms if a star cannot get hot enough to reach nuclear fusion. It failed to become a proper star but is still not a planet because it does glow dimly.

- As yellow dwarf stars like our Sun start to run out of hydrogen fuel, the core shrinks, heats, and pushes out the rest of the star turning it into a red giant.

- Red supergiants, such as Betelgeuse in the constellation Orion make our Sun look small, 20x its mass, and 1,000x larger. Red hypergiants such as the largest known star VY Canis Majoris are even bigger, over 1,800x the size of the Sun.

- When smaller stars such as red dwarfs or red giants use up all their fuel and nuclear fusion slows, they start to die and become small "white dwarf" stars which emit white light until they finally darken into "black dwarfs".

o Big stars like supergiants and hypergiants have shorter lives as they consume their fuel at a faster rate than smaller stars. As these massive stars die, they explode as massive bright supernovas.

o Very heavy stars that have gone supernova can turn into black holes.

o Other supernovae leave behind very small, 20 to 40km (25 mi) in diameter, white neutron stars that have dense cores made of neutrons.

o Star matter blown away by supernova explosions form new stellar nebula and the process of making stars begins again.

o Stars range in color depending on how hot they are, in order from lowest to highest temperature they can be brown, red, orange, yellow, white, or blue.

o The light from stars takes millions of years to reach Earth, therefore when you look at the stars you are looking back in time.

o Stars do not twinkle. They only appear to twinkle due to turbulences in the Earth's atmosphere deflecting the light that reaches our eyes.

o The stars have played a very important role throughout human history.

o They have formed part of religious practices, been grouped into constellations, used in astrology star signs, helped to design calendars, and were very important navigational tools for early explorations across land and seas.

o Stars shine bright and then fade away. But when they explode in a brilliant supernova, they scatter life-building elements into space. Those elements go on to form new stars, planets, and even us.

o The North Star, or Polaris, remains nearly stationary in the sky as other stars seem to rotate around it.

o There are icy objects far away from the Sun called comets. When they get closer to the Sun, they grow a glowing tail that points away from it.

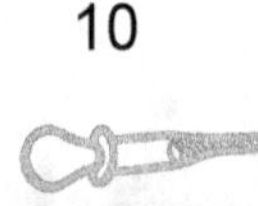

THE MOON

- Earth's moon is gradually moving away from us! Billions of years from now, the moon might just be very far from us.

- Like Earth, the Moon has gravity (the force that pulls things towards the ground). But the Moon's gravity is weaker, only one-sixth of the Earth's gravity. That means you'd weigh much less if you were to stand on the Moon!

- If you could drive a car all the way to the Moon, it would take you about 6 months to get there if you drove non stop at 60 miles per hour!

- It takes 27.3 days for the Moon to travel around the Earth and complete its orbit.

- The temperature on the Moon varies from super hot to super cold! When the Sun hits its surface, temperatures can reach a scorching But when the Sun 'goes down', temperatures can plummet to around -153°C.

- Although the Moon shines bright in the night sky, it doesn't produce its own light. We see the Moon because it reflects light from the Sun.

- Ever noticed how the Moon appears to change shape each night? That's because as the Moon orbits the Earth, the Sun lights up different parts of its surface – so it's just our view of the Moon that's changing, not the Moon itself.

- Scientists aren't entirely sure how the Moon formed. A popular theory is that a Mars-sized rock, named Theia, crashed into Earth around 4.5 billion years ago. The debris from the collision clumped together to make what is now... Our Moon!

- The Moon has no atmosphere but is dusty and has a rough surface.

- The Moon has large and wide craters, mountains, and planes made of lava. These craters are said to be made by various asteroid collisions.

- The tallest mountain on the Moon is called Mons Huygens. It is 4,700 meters high (approximately half the height of Mt. Everest in the Himalayas).

- The largest crater on the Moon is called Bailly. It covers a surface area of 26 square miles.

- The Moon is the only object in our Solar System to have been physically visited by a human.

- The Moon's surface area is the size of the African continent.

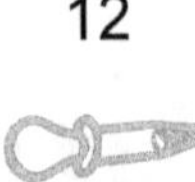

THE PLANETS

- Imagine a languid dance on the planet Venus, where a day lasts longer than a year. This rocky world takes about 225 Earth days to orbit the Sun but rotates at a sluggish pace, making its day approximately 243 Earth days long.

- Mars has lower gravity than Earth. That means a person that weighs 200 pounds on Earth would only weigh 76 pounds on Mars.

- Jupiter, the mighty gas giant, isn't just large - it's got a voice too. Its massive storms create thunder that's not like the rumble we're used to on Earth. If you could hear it, you'd be listening to a cosmic symphony of booming echoes.

- Neptune, the ice giant, is home to the fastest winds in our solar system. It reaches a speed of 1200 miles per hour.

- Jupiter is the fastest spinning planet in the solar system.

- The largest planet in our solar system, Jupiter, is a cosmic giant that could accommodate over 1,300 Earths within its voluminous boundaries. It also boasts a grand retinue of over 80 moons, each with its own story to tell.

- There's a planet named Venus that's so hot it can melt lead! That makes it hotter than the planet Mercury, which is closest to the Sun. Venus is the hottest planet in our solar system due to its thick atmosphere trapping heat.

- The planet Uranus spins on its side, so it's like it is rolling along as it orbits the Sun.

o The largest volcano in the solar system isn't on Earth, it's on Mars! It's called Olympus Mons and it's about 13.6 miles (22 kilometers) high.

o The moon Io, which is one of Jupiter's moons, has more than 400 active volcanoes!

o The planet Saturn is famous for its stunning rings made up of icy particles and rocks.

o If you weighed 100 pounds on Earth, you would weigh only about 38 pounds on the planet Mars due to its weaker gravity.

o If you looked at the night sky from Mars, you'd see two tiny moons called Phobos and Deimos, which are much smaller than Earth's moon.

o The farthest planet from the Sun is Neptune, and it's so far away that sunlight takes about 4 hours to reach it!

o Some planets, like Earth, have a moon, while others have many! Jupiter has over 80 moons.

o The solar system also has many moons. Now, we all know that our planet has one moon, but did you know that Jupiter has more than 60? Other planets to have several moons are Saturn, Uranus, and Neptune. The biggest moon in the system is Ganymede and it is a satellite of Jupiter.

SPACE TRAVEL

- During the Apollo 13 mission, astronauts voyaged about 248,655 miles from Earth – the farthest humans have ventured. This odyssey stands as a testament to human determination and exploration beyond our planet's borders.

- While most of us think the Earth is shaped like a large sphere, it actually looks more like a "squashed ball" that bulges out at the equator. We can thank gravity for that!

- Astronauts have to exercise a lot in space to keep their muscles strong because without gravity, their muscles would become weak.

- The German V2 was the first rocket to reach space in 1942.

- Later, in 1949, Albert II, a Rhesus monkey went to space. In 1957, the Russian space dog, Laika, orbited the Earth.

- In 1959, the Russian spacecraft, Luna 2, landed on the moon. It crashed at high speed. Fortunately, it was an unmanned craft with no astronauts inside.

- Russian astronaut, Yuri Gagarin, was the first human in space. He orbited the Earth in 1961.

- On July 20, 1969, Neil Armstrong and Buzz Aldrin became the first men to walk on the moon and return home safely – a journey of 250,000 miles.

- 1981 marked the first space shuttle that could be used again. Six shuttles have been built since then.

- Since 2000, permanent crews have been living and working in space at the International Space Station.

- In 2001, the first private citizen, millionaire Dennis Tito, toured space. He paid $20 million to spend a week in space.

- Space stations, like the International Space Station (ISS), orbit Earth and serve as scientific laboratories where astronauts conduct experiments, study the effects of space on the human body, and collaborate with researchers from around the world.

- Astronauts sometimes go on spacewalks outside of their spacecraft or space station. These spacewalks, or extravehicular activities (EVAs), allow astronauts to repair equipment, install new instruments, and perform maintenance tasks.

- Not all space travel involves humans. Robotic spacecraft, such as rovers and probes, have explored other planets and moons in our solar system, sending back valuable data and images.

- Rovers like Spirit, Opportunity, and Curiosity have roamed the Martian surface, analyzing rocks and soil to learn more about the planet's history and potential for past life.

- The Voyager 1 spacecraft was launched in 1977 and is now the farthest human-made object from Earth. It's exploring the outer regions of our solar system and beyond.

- Some companies are working on space tourism, offering civilians the chance to experience weightlessness and see the Earth from space. This could open up space travel to people who aren't professional astronauts.

- For a rocket to get into orbit around Earth, it needs to travel 17,600 miles per hour!

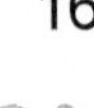

- As technology advances, the dream of sending humans to other planets, like Mars, becomes more achievable. NASA's Artemis program aims to return humans to the Moon and eventually send astronauts to Mars.

- Re-entering the atmosphere is dangerous too. When a space craft re-enters the atmosphere, it is moving very fast. As it moves through the air, friction causes it to heat up to a temperature of 2,691 degrees. The first spacecrafts were destroyed during re-entry. Today's space shuttles have special ceramic tiles that help absorb some of the heat, keeping the astronauts safe during re-entry.

- Astronauts Grow Taller in Space. Due to the absence of gravity's downward pull, astronauts can experience a growth spurt of up to 2 inches while in space. Unfortunately, they return to their normal height upon returning to Earth.

- Stars seem close, don't they? If you were traveling at almost 12,500 miles per hour on a space shuttle, it would still take you 165,000 years to reach the closest star in our galaxy.

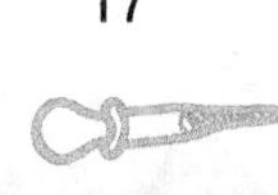

AMAZING
PLACES

BUILDINGS

- The Great Sphinx of Giza in Egypt has the body of a lion and the head of a pharaoh.

- The Shanghai Tower in China is a modern skyscraper notable for its twisting design. It stands as a symbol of innovative architecture and sustainable construction practices.

- The Pyramids of Giza were built more than 4,500 years ago and are some of the oldest structures on Earth.

- The Great Wall of China was built over centuries to protect against invasions and is around 13,170 miles (21,196 kilometers) long.

- Petra in Jordan is a city carved into pink rock cliffs and was the capital of the Nabatean Kingdom over 2,000 years ago.

- The Roman Colosseum could hold around 50,000 spectators and hosted gladiator battles and other events.

- The Statue of Liberty in the USA was a gift from France, and it's like a big, green welcome sign for people coming to America.

- The Eiffel Tower is one of the most recognizable landmarks globally, and it was completed in 1889 as the entrance arch for the 1889 World's Fair.

- The Taj Mahal is a breathtaking white marble mausoleum located in Agra, India. It was built in the 17th century by Emperor Shah Jahan in memory of his wife Mumtaz Mahal.

- The Burj Khalifa is a towering skyscraper in Dubai, United Arab Emirates. It stands as the tallest building in the world, with a height of over 2,700 feet.

- The Parthenon is an ancient temple located on the Acropolis of Athens, Greece. It was constructed in the 5th century BC and dedicated to the goddess Athena.

- The Sydney Opera House is a modern architectural masterpiece situated in Sydney, Australia. Its distinctive sail-like design has made it an iconic symbol of the city.

- The Petronas Towers are twin skyscrapers in Kuala Lumpur, Malaysia. They held the title of the world's tallest buildings from 1998 to 2004.

- The Louvre Pyramid is an iconic glass pyramid entrance to the Louvre Museum in Paris, France. It serves as a striking contrast to the museum's historic architecture.

- The Golden Gate Bridge is a renowned suspension bridge in San Francisco, California, USA. It spans the Golden Gate Strait, connecting San Francisco to Marin County.

- Hagia Sophia, located in Istanbul, Turkey, has a rich history as a cathedral, mosque, and museum. It stands as a testament to the architectural and cultural heritage of the region.

- The Leaning Tower of Pisa, situated in Pisa, Italy, is known for its distinctive tilt. Despite its unintended angle, it has become a popular tourist attraction.

- Machu Picchu is an ancient Incan city located in the Andes Mountains of Peru. Its remarkable preservation and stunning location have made it a UNESCO World Heritage Site.

- The Shanghai Tower in China is a modern skyscraper notable for its twisting design. It stands as a symbol of innovative architecture and sustainable construction practices.

COUNTRIES AND CONTINENTS

- The Cappadocia region in Turkey is famous for its "fairy chimneys," tall rock formations formed by volcanic eruptions.

- The Wave in Arizona, USA, is a sandstone rock formation that looks like an ocean wave frozen in time.

- Asia is the largest continent on earth. This also means it has the largest population with over 4.46 billion people!

- The Grand Canyon is the largest canyon in the world. Located in Arizona, it is massive, with an elevation of 2,600 feet and a length of 277 miles.

- Russia is just 2 miles from Alaska. Who would've thought they'd be so close? Crazy!

- The country of Brazil is so big that it's almost as big as the entire continent of Europe!

- The city of Dubai in the United Arab Emirates is like a modern desert oasis with towering skyscrapers and luxurious buildings.

- The United States and Canada share the longest border in the world. In total, it spans over 1,538 miles!

- The Northern Lights, or Aurora Borealis, are colorful lights that dance in the sky near the North Pole.

- The country of Greece is famous for its ancient ruins and stories about powerful gods and goddesses.

- Australia is a country and a whole continent by itself! It's also home to lots of unique animals like kangaroos and koalas.

- Did you know that there's a country named after a bird? It's called Turkey, and it's located partly in Europe and partly in Asia.

- The city of Venice in Italy is so unique because it's built on water and has canals instead of roads.

- There's a country called Iceland, but it's not all icy! And another country called Greenland, which has a lot of ice.

- Madagascar is an island country with a treasure chest of amazing animals you won't find anywhere else, like lemurs.

- Japan is made up of many islands, and it's famous for its delicious sushi and beautiful cherry blossoms.

- The smallest country in the world is Vatican City, which is like a tiny country inside the city of Rome, Italy.

- Norway is a country where you might see the Northern Lights in the sky, which are colorful dancing lights.

- The country of Egypt has a river called the Nile, and most of the people live close to it because the land around the river is fertile and good for farming.

- The Netherlands is a country where some people live below sea level, and they've built walls called dikes to keep the water out.

- New Zealand is a country where you can find amazing things such as geysers, which shoot hot water and steam high into the air.

- Russia is the largest country in the world and spans two continents, Europe and Asia.

- The Galápagos Islands in the Pacific Ocean are home to animals that you won't find anywhere else, like giant tortoises and blue-footed boobies.

- Did you know that there's a country inside another country? It's called Lesotho, and it's like a puzzle piece inside South Africa.

ISLANDS

- Hawaii is a group of volcanic islands located in the Pacific Ocean. Mauna Kea, a dormant volcano on the Big Island, is one of the best places on Earth for stargazing.

- Madagascar is the fourth-largest island in the world and is known for its diverse wildlife, including lemurs found nowhere else on Earth.

- The Maldives is an archipelago of over 1,000 coral islands in the Indian Ocean. It's famous for its stunning turquoise waters and luxurious overwater bungalows.

- Iceland is a volcanic island nation in the North Atlantic. It's known for its geothermal energy, geysers, hot springs, and stunning landscapes.

- The Galápagos Islands are located off the coast of Ecuador and are known for their unique and diverse wildlife that inspired Charles Darwin's theory of evolution.

- Bora Bora is a small island in French Polynesia known for its turquoise lagoon and luxurious resorts. It's a popular honeymoon destination.

- Santorini is a Greek island famous for its white-washed buildings with blue domes and stunning sunsets over the Aegean Sea.

- Jeju Island is a volcanic island in South Korea and is known for its beautiful beaches, lava tubes, and unique "haenyeo" female divers.

- New Zealand is made up of two main islands, the North Island and the South Island. The country is known for its breathtaking landscapes, including mountains, fjords, and geothermal areas.

- Easter Island is a remote island in the Pacific Ocean known for its iconic moai statues, massive stone sculptures that were carved by the Rapa Nui people.

- Despite its name, Greenland is covered mostly by ice. It's an autonomous territory of Denmark and is known for its stunning Arctic landscapes.

- Seychelles is an archipelago in the Indian Ocean known for its white sandy beaches, clear waters, and diverse marine life.

- Komodo Island in Indonesia is home to the famous Komodo dragons, the world's largest lizards.

- Ibiza is a party hotspot in the Mediterranean Sea, famous for its vibrant nightlife and beautiful beaches.

- Manhattan is an island in New York City, known for its iconic skyline, Central Park, and cultural landmarks.

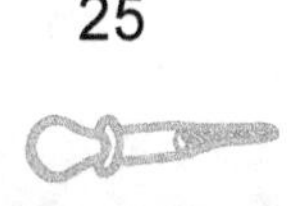

DESERTS

- Some desert sand dunes can produce a musical sound, known as "singing" or "booming" sand. When the grains of sand slide down the dune, they create a resonating vibration that produces a humming or even a booming noise, like a low-pitched note from a musical instrument.

- Deserts are famous for mirages, where distant objects appear to be closer or even inverted due to the bending of light. This optical illusion can be so convincing that it has often been mistaken for water.

- "Rain" in the Desert: Some deserts experience infrequent rainfall, but when it does rain, it can be quite intense. Flash floods are common in desert regions, as the dry ground cannot absorb the water quickly enough, leading to sudden and powerful flows.

- Contrary to the barren image of deserts, some deserts experience "superblooms" where after a rare, heavy rain, the desert floor explodes with colorful wildflowers in a stunning display of beauty.

- Deserts are known for their extreme temperature fluctuations between day and night. In some deserts, the temperature can drop dramatically after sunset, leading to very cold nights despite the daytime heat.

- The desert is home to remarkable species such as the "Welwitschia," a plant found in the Namib Desert that can live for over 1,000 years. It consists of just two leaves that grow continuously throughout its lifetime.

o Some desert creatures have incredible adaptations to survive in the arid environment. The kangaroo rat, for example, gets almost all the water it needs from its food and can go its entire life without drinking water.

o Due to the angle of the sun during sunrise and sunset, desert landscapes can create long shadows and make objects appear stretched out and distorted, resulting in surreal and almost otherworldly views.

o Some deserts, like the Salar de Uyuni in Bolivia, have expansive salt flats that create a mirror effect after rain. When covered by a thin layer of water, the flats perfectly reflect the sky, creating a stunning optical illusion.

o While deserts might seem desolate, they actually host a wide variety of life adapted to survive in harsh conditions, including camels, scorpions, and rattlesnakes.

o In some desert regions, ancient artifacts and petroglyphs (rock carvings) reveal the history and stories of past civilizations, providing valuable insights into the people who once inhabited these areas.

o Oases are lush spots within deserts, often formed around natural springs. These oases have provided crucial water sources for travelers and wildlife for centuries.

o The Sahara Desert in Africa is so vast that it's roughly the size of the entire United States.

o The hottest desert in the world is the Sahara desert. Located in Africa, the average temperature is around 30°C (86°F), but the hottest temperature ever recorded is 58°C (136.4°F).

- The Atacama Desert in Chile is often considered the driest desert on Earth, with some areas having not received any significant rainfall for hundreds of years.

- Antarctica is the world's largest cold desert, with extremely low temperatures and very little precipitation. It's covered by ice and snow.

- The Gobi Desert in Asia spans both northern China and southern Mongolia. It's known for its vast sand dunes and harsh climate.

- The Sonoran Desert in North America extends across parts of Arizona, California, and Mexico. It's home to the iconic saguaro cactus.

- The Namib Desert in Namibia is famous for its towering sand dunes, some of which are among the tallest in the world.

- The Arabian Desert covers much of the Arabian Peninsula and is known for its vast stretches of sand and extreme temperatures.

- The Mojave Desert is located in the southwestern United States and is home to unique desert flora and fauna, including the Joshua tree.

- The Kalahari Desert spans parts of Botswana, Namibia, and South Africa. It's not a "true" desert as it receives slightly more rainfall.

- The Colorado Plateau in the United States is a high desert region characterized by canyons, mesas, and unique rock formations like those in Bryce Canyon and Zion National Park.

o One-third of the Earth's surface is barren land or desert land.

o The Great Victoria Desert is located in Australia and is known for its vast and remote landscapes.

o The Chihuahuan Desert covers parts of the southwestern United States and northern Mexico. It's the largest desert in North America.

o The Karakum Desert in Central Asia is home to the famous Darvaza Gas Crater, often referred to as the "Door to Hell."

o Animals and plants living in the deserts have adapted to the environment. Animals usually are night active and live in burrows underground six as the cajole or the fennel fox. Some animals receive their water intake from the fog in coastal deserts or store water in humps such as the camel. Desert plants often have deep roots and waxy leaves where they can store water and often they also have thorns such as cacti to deter herbivores, animals that eat plants.

o After it rains once, a desert might not get rain again for months or even years.

o Deserts get cold at night because of a lack of humidity. They don't have clouds and water vapor to hold in heat like other places.

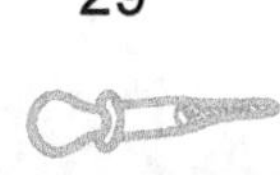

FORESTS

- The Amazon Rainforest in South America is bigger than the whole United States!

- Forests play a vital role in producing oxygen and absorbing carbon dioxide through photosynthesis, making them essential for maintaining the Earth's oxygen balance and mitigating climate change.

- Some of the tallest and oldest living organisms on Earth are found in forests. Giant sequoias and coastal redwoods can live for thousands of years and reach incredible heights, with some trees taller than a 30-story building!

- Forests are home to an incredible array of plant and animal species. Tropical rainforests, for example, contain over half of the world's known plant and animal species, making them biodiversity hotspots.

- The forest floor is teeming with life, from tiny insects and fungi to larger mammals and birds. Many plants that grow on the forest floor have evolved unique adaptations to survive in the limited sunlight and competition for resources.

- The treetops of forests create what is known as the "canopy layer." This upper layer is like a hidden world filled with wildlife, including birds, monkeys, and insects that seldom come down to the forest floor.

- Forests are a treasure trove of medicinal plants. Many traditional medicines are derived from plants found in forests, and indigenous communities have used these remedies for generations.

o Rainforests, especially tropical rainforests, play a significant role in regulating the Earth's water cycle. They release moisture through a process called transpiration, which can influence weather patterns around the world.

o Indigenous cultures around the world have deep connections to forests, often valuing them for their spiritual and cultural significance. Many indigenous communities have traditional knowledge about forest ecosystems that has been passed down for generations.

o Despite their importance, forests face threats from deforestation due to logging, agriculture, and urban expansion. Deforestation not only disrupts ecosystems but also contributes to climate change.

o Forests are known for their symphony of sounds, from the chirping of insects to the calls of birds and the rustling of leaves. Some forests can be surprisingly quiet, while others resonate with a cacophony of life.

o Temperate forests, found in regions with distinct seasons, experience dramatic changes throughout the year. Trees shed their leaves in the fall, creating vibrant displays of colors, and then regrow them in the spring.

o Forests are interconnected ecosystems where plants, animals, and microorganisms rely on each other for survival. The relationships between different species create intricate food webs and nutrient cycles.

o While forest fires can be devastating, they also play an essential role in forest ecosystems. Some tree species have evolved to rely on fires to release seeds or clear space for new growth.

Forests provide us with valuable resources like wood, fruits, nuts, and medicinal plants. Sustainable forest management is crucial to ensure these resources are available for future generations.

RIVERS LAKES AND WATERFALLS

- The Nile River is widely accepted as the world's longest river. Found in north Africa, it flows through 11 different countries and stretches a whopping 6,695km – that's as long as 65,000 football pitches!

- Most scientists agree that the Amazon River comes in a close second, winding a huge 6,840km through the mountains and rainforests of South America!

- But what about the world's deepest river? That's the Congo River in Central Africa. Whilst its true depth remains a mystery, scientists believe the waters run at least 230m deep in parts – deep enough to submerge London's famous clocktower, known as Big Ben, 2.5 times on top of each other!

- As rivers flow their course across the land, they form lots of fascinating geographic features, such as amazing mountain valleys, canyons, lakes and, of course, wonderful waterfalls!

- The Dead Sea, located between Jordan and Israel, is so salty that you can float on its surface without even trying.

- The Great Lakes in North America are so big that they look like huge oceans, and you can't see the other side when you're standing on the shore.

- The world's tallest waterfall, Angel Falls in Venezuela, is so high that the water almost turns into mist before it hits the ground.

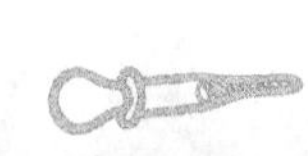

- Not all rivers flow overland – 'subterranean rivers' run secretly beneath the surface! This is sometimes because of human engineering. Ever heard of London's 'lost rivers'? These are streams of the River Thames and River Lea that were built over as the city grew.

- Subterranean rivers can also exist naturally. In the Philippines for example, the Puerto Princesa Underground River flows beneath a mountain for five miles, before finally emptying into the South China Sea. Cool, eh?

- It's not just rivers themselves which are fascinating – it's the wonderful wildlife that lives in them, too! Rivers provide a home for all kinds of creatures, including insects, amphibians, birds, reptiles, mammals and over 10,000 species of fish!

- Some of the most fascinating river creatures include Amazon river dolphins (which have pink skin!), electric eels (which stun prey and predators with powerful electric shocks!), freshwater stingrays (which can grow to an enormous 5 metres!) and freshwater turtles, which have been around for 200 million years!

- A waterfall is a location along a watercourse where water flows over a vertical drop.

- They typically appear along the upper part of a watercourse where higher elevations and mountains are found and create the right conditions for a waterfall.

- Waterfalls are created by the erosion process. Sediment in water can erode soft bedrock and overtime it will completely erode all the soft bedrock until only harder rocks remain.

- o A manmade lake or artificial lake is a body of water created by humans and typically called a reservoir.

- o Reservoirs are used by humans as a source of drinking water, power generation and/or recreational activities.

- o Droughts and human activity have caused some lakes to dry up and disappear forever.

- o Lake Chad was one of the largest lakes in Africa. However, between 1963 and 1998 activities by humans caused Lake Chad to shrink up to 95%.

- o The largest freshwater lake in the world by surface area is Lake Superior. Lake Superior covers around 31,700 square miles.

- o The largest freshwater lake in the world by volume is Lake Baikal in Siberia, Russia. Lake Baikal holds around 5,670 cubic miles of water.

- o The largest freshwater lake in the world by length is Lake Tanganyika in Tanzania, Africa.

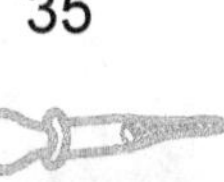

MOUNTAINS AND VOLCANOES

- Mount Everest, the tallest mountain on Earth, grows about 4 millimeters each year due to tectonic forces.

- Hawaii's Mauna Loa is the largest active volcano in the world.

- The Andes in South America are the longest mountain range in the world.

- The Earth's highest point, Mount Everest, is so tall that you could fit more than 19 Statues of Liberty stacked on top of each other to reach its peak.

- Mount Fuji in Japan is a perfectly shaped volcano that's famous for its snowy top.

- The Andes Mountains in South America are so tall that they have some of the highest places on Earth, like the city of La Paz, Bolivia.

- Mount Kilimanjaro in Tanzania is the tallest mountain in Africa and has a snowy peak even though it's near the equator.

- Volcanic eruptions can vary widely in their intensity. Some eruptions release a steady flow of lava, while others can result in explosive blasts that shoot ash, rock fragments, and gasses into the sky.

- Mountains are typically formed by tectonic forces pushing, folding, and uplifting the Earth's crust. The collision of tectonic plates can result in the formation of mountain ranges like the Alps or the Rockies.

- Around 10% of the world's population lives in or near areas vulnerable to volcanic eruptions. While volcanic soil is fertile, these regions also face the risks of lava flows, ash clouds, and pyroclastic flows.

- Volcanic soil is incredibly fertile due to the minerals released during eruptions. This type of soil supports lush vegetation and has contributed to the development of thriving agricultural communities.

- Mountains attract adventurers and hikers seeking breathtaking views and challenging climbs. Mount Kilimanjaro in Tanzania is a popular trekking destination, and some people climb it to see the sunrise from its summit.

- Many high mountain peaks are capped with glaciers. These frozen rivers of ice shape the landscape and provide a vital water source for downstream communities.

- Layers of rock in mountains and volcanoes can reveal clues about Earth's history. Geologists study these layers to understand past climates, ancient ecosystems, and even the movement of continents.

- The Pacific Ring of Fire is responsible for some of the most powerful volcanic eruptions in history. The eruption of Mount Tambora in Indonesia in 1815, known as the "Year Without a Summer," led to global climate anomalies.

- Some of the world's most famous islands, like Hawaii and the Galápagos Islands, are volcanic in origin. These islands formed as lava accumulated and cooled over time.

- Volcanic activity is a natural process that contributes to the creation of new land. Islands and landmasses continue to form as molten rock rises from the Earth's mantle and solidifies at the surface.

OCEANS

- The Great Barrier Reef in Australia is like a giant underwater city made of colorful coral, and it's the only living thing that you can see from space.

- The oceans cover about 71% of Earth's surface, containing approximately 97% of its water.

- The Mariana Trench in the Pacific Ocean is the deepest part of any ocean, plunging to over 36,000 feet (10,994 meters).

- The average depth of the oceans is around 12,080 feet (3,682 meters).

- The Blue Whale, the largest animal on Earth, lives in the ocean and can weigh as much as 200 tons.

- Earth's longest mountain range, the Mid-Ocean Ridge, stretches for more than 40,000 miles (64,000 kilometers) underwater.

- The ocean contains approximately 20 million tons of gold dissolved in its waters.

- The "Twilight Zone" of the ocean, also called the mesopelagic zone, is where sunlight barely reaches and many unique and bizarre creatures live.

- The deepest parts of the ocean remain largely unexplored, with more people having walked on the moon than ventured to the bottom of the Mariana Trench.

- The pressure at the bottom of the Mariana Trench is over 1,000 times greater than at sea level.

- o Earth's largest mountain, Mauna Kea in Hawaii, is actually an underwater mountain, with most of its mass submerged.

- o More people have explored space than have dived into the deep oceans.

- o The ocean is a massive carbon sink, absorbing and storing large amounts of carbon dioxide.

- o The ocean's saltiness comes from minerals eroded from rocks on land and carried into the sea by rivers.

- o The ocean's tides are primarily caused by the gravitational pull of the Moon.

- o The Challenger Deep, located in the Mariana Trench, is the lowest point on Earth's surface.

- o Seaweed, which is a type of algae, can grow over 150 feet (46 meters) long in the ocean.

- o The ocean produces over half of the world's oxygen through photosynthesis by marine plants like phytoplankton.

- o Some species of sharks can sense electrical fields generated by other creatures, helping them locate prey.

- o The "ocean conveyor belt" is a global circulation system that helps regulate Earth's climate by distributing heat around the planet.

- o The ocean holds ancient shipwrecks and underwater cities, preserving history beneath its waves.

- o The Pacific Ocean is so large that it could fit all of Earth's landmasses with room to spare.

o Sunlight can only penetrate around 660 feet (200 meters) into the ocean, beyond which it's completely dark.

o The ocean's temperature decreases with depth, and some areas have cold seeps with unique ecosystems.

o The ocean contains more artifacts and treasures than all of the world's museums combined.

o Some areas of the ocean floor are covered in hydrothermal vents, where superheated water gushes out, supporting unique ecosystems.

o The ocean's salinity can vary based on location, depth, and local conditions.

o The "Dumbo Octopus" is a rare and adorable octopus species named after the Disney character due to its ear-like fins.

o The ocean's currents help distribute heat around the globe, influencing weather patterns and climate.

o The largest coral reef, the Great Barrier Reef, is so big it can even be seen from the Moon.

o The Sargasso Sea in the North Atlantic is the only sea without a land boundary.

o The ocean's "dead zones" are areas with low oxygen levels, often caused by pollution runoff from land.

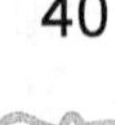

THE WEATHER

- Hailstones can range in size from tiny pellets to as large as baseballs, depending on the strength of the storm.

- The highest temperature ever recorded on Earth was 134°F (56.7°C) in Furnace Creek Ranch, Death Valley, USA.

- The world's wettest place is Mawsynram, India, where it can rain over 467 inches (11,871 millimeters) a year

- The driest place on Earth is the Atacama Desert in Chile, where some areas haven't seen rain for hundreds of years.

- Did you know there are nearly 2,000 thunderstorms on Earth every minute?

- Clouds look white because they are reflecting sunlight from above them.

- A bolt of lightning is five times hotter than the sun!!

- The fastest recorded raindrop traveled at 18 mph!

- Did you know that you can estimate the temperature of a place by the number of times some crickets chirp in a second? Weird but true!!

- An avalanche can travel up to 80 mph!

- While we typically see rainbows as arcs, they are actually full circles. When viewed from an airplane or high altitude, you can see the complete circle of a rainbow.

- The largest hailstone ever recorded weighed around 2.25 pounds (1 kg) and had a diameter of 8 inches (20 cm). It fell in Vivian, South Dakota, in 2010.

- The pleasant earthy smell that often follows a rainstorm is called "petrichor." It's caused by the release of oils from plants and the soil into the air.

- Lightning strikes the Earth's surface around 100 times per second. That adds up to over 8 million lightning strikes per day!

- The widest tornado ever recorded occurred in El Reno, Oklahoma, in 2013. It reached a width of 2.6 miles (4.2 km).

- The windiest spot on Earth is often considered to be Commonwealth Bay in Antarctica. Wind speeds can reach over 150 miles per hour (240 km/h) on a regular basis.

- Lightning can be incredibly hot—reaching temperatures hotter than the surface of the Sun. At the same time, it cools very quickly and can create a shock wave that results in thunder.

- Changes in weather can influence your mood and behavior. Some people experience increased happiness and energy on sunny days, while others may feel more lethargic during overcast weather.

- Microbursts are intense, localized downdrafts that can create sudden and powerful winds. These winds can be as strong as those in a small tornado and are a hazard to aviation.

- The saying "Red sky at night, sailor's delight; red sky in the morning, sailor's warning" has some meteorological truth. A red sky at sunset can indicate that high pressure and fair weather are on the way, while a red sky in the morning can indicate an approaching low-pressure system and potential rain.

o   No two snowflakes are exactly alike due to the complex process of ice crystal formation in clouds. Each snowflake takes on a unique shape as it grows.

o   Thunderstorms produce gamma-ray bursts that can be more energetic than a million nuclear bombs. These bursts create high-energy particles that can interfere with spacecraft and satellites.

o   Some animals can predict weather changes. For instance, cows often lie down before a storm arrives, and birds might fly lower to the ground in response to low pressure.

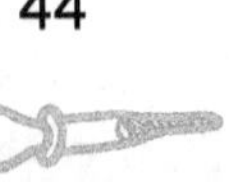

THE PAST

HISTORICAL CURIOSITIES

- In 1992, after a record amount of snow, the government of Syracuse, NY, declared any additional snowfall before Christmas Eve illegal.

- Unfortunately, Mother Nature didn't take the threat too seriously. It snowed two days after the move was announced.

- Ketchup used to be sold as medicine. That's right; the popular condiment was once thought to be a cure for indigestion.

- Abraham Lincoln was once declared a wrestling champion. He was also a licensed bartender

- The Inca Empire in South America ingeniously used a system of knotted cords known as quipus for record-keeping. These intricate knots held information about everything from trade to census data.

- The Silk Road was a network of trade routes that connected the East and West, facilitating the exchange of goods, ideas, and cultures between civilizations spanning from China to the Mediterranean.

- The Moai statues of Easter Island are a mystery that captivates the imagination. Carved by the Rapa Nui people, these massive stone figures are a testament to their artistic skill and engineering prowess.

- A lot of Viking men actually dyed their hair blonde. Some even dyed their beards as well!

o In Australia in 1932, a bizarre event known as the "Great Emu War" took place. Farmers requested help from the military to deal with emus damaging their crops. The military was sent to fight the emus using machine guns, but the emus proved surprisingly difficult to defeat.

o In 1518, a strange phenomenon known as the "Dancing Plague" occurred in Strasbourg, France. Hundreds of people began dancing uncontrollably and couldn't stop, some even dancing until they collapsed from exhaustion.

o The Voynich Manuscript is a mysterious medieval book filled with strange drawings and an indecipherable script. To this day, its origin, purpose, and content remain a mystery, intriguing historians and cryptographers.

o In the 17th century, the Netherlands experienced a financial bubble known as "Tulip Mania." People went to extreme lengths to buy tulip bulbs, with prices soaring to absurd levels. The bubble eventually burst, leaving many in financial ruin.

o In the late 19th century, the bicycle gained popularity, and a curious phenomenon called "bicycle face" was reported. It was believed that excessive cycling could lead to facial distortions and health issues, causing public concern.

o In 1839, Robert Cornelius took what is considered the first photographic self-portrait, or "selfie," by standing still for several minutes in front of his camera.

o Some people around the world claim to hear a mysterious and unexplainable low-frequency humming noise called "the Hum." Despite efforts to identify its source, its origin remains elusive.

- In Russia during the reign of Peter the Great, a "beard tax" was imposed on men with beards. Those who refused to pay were required to carry a token indicating they had paid the tax. This tax was part of Peter's efforts to modernize Russia.

- In 1919, a storage tank containing molasses burst in Boston, leading to a wave of molasses flooding the streets at a high speed. The incident resulted in several deaths and significant damage, earning it the nickname the "Great Molasses Flood."

- In 1788, during the Austro-Turkish War, Austrian forces accidentally attacked their own troops while intoxicated, resulting in chaos and a significant number of casualties. The battle is often cited as an example of miscommunication and poor leadership.

- The iconic Leaning Tower of Pisa began leaning during its construction due to the unstable ground. Builders attempted to compensate for the tilt, resulting in the distinctive slant that has puzzled and intrigued visitors for centuries.

ANTIQUITY

- The Indus Valley Civilization had advanced sewage and drainage systems over 4,000 years ago.

- The Roman Colosseum could hold around 50,000 spectators and hosted gladiator battles and other events.

- The ancient city of Pompeii was buried by the eruption of Mount Vesuvius in 79 AD, preserving its buildings and artifacts.

- The Mayans used a system of hieroglyphs to write and record information.

- The ancient city of Carthage, located in present-day Tunisia, was a powerful maritime civilization that rivaled the Roman Empire. The Punic Wars between Rome and Carthage were epic conflicts that shaped the course of history.

- The Library of Alexandria in ancient Egypt was a marvel of knowledge, housing a vast collection of scrolls and texts from across the ancient world. Its destruction remains a tragic loss to human history.

- The ancient Greeks had a rich tradition of competitive sports, leading to the creation of the Olympic Games. These early Olympics featured events like chariot racing, wrestling, and discus throwing.

- The ancient Greeks held the first Olympic Games in 776 BCE in Olympia. These athletic contests honored the god Zeus and showcased physical prowess and sportsmanship.

- The Mausoleum at Halicarnassus, built in honor of a Carian princess, was one of the Seven Wonders of the Ancient World. This ornate tomb blended Greek and Egyptian architectural styles.

- Writing systems emerged independently in various ancient civilizations. The Sumerians in Mesopotamia developed cuneiform, while the Egyptians created hieroglyphs, marking the birth of recorded history.

- The ancient Egyptians built awe-inspiring pyramids, such as the Great Pyramid of Giza. These monumental structures served as tombs for pharaohs and were constructed with remarkable precision.

- Ancient Greece was home to great thinkers like Socrates, Plato, and Aristotle. Their philosophical inquiries laid the foundation for Western philosophy and continue to influence modern thought.

- The ancient Greeks held the first Olympic Games in 776 BCE in Olympia. These athletic contests honored the god Zeus and showcased physical prowess and sportsmanship.

- The Roman Empire, spanning three continents, brought advancements in engineering, governance, and law. The Roman Republic transformed into an empire under the rule of Julius Caesar and his successors.

- The Silk Road connected civilizations across Asia, facilitating the exchange of goods, ideas, and cultures. This trade network facilitated the spread of inventions, religions, and artistic styles.

- The Library of Alexandria in ancient Egypt was renowned for its collection of scrolls and texts, making it a center of learning and scholarship in antiquity.

- The "Epic of Gilgamesh," an ancient Mesopotamian poem, is among the earliest known works of literature. It explores themes of mortality, friendship, and the quest for wisdom.

- The achievements of antiquity continue to influence modern societies. Concepts of democracy, philosophy, architecture, and law have been shaped by the wisdom of ancient civilizations.

EXPLORERS

- In 1492, Christopher Columbus, an Italian explorer, set sail on a daring journey to find a new route to Asia. Instead, he reached a new land, the Americas. His voyage changed the course of history, connecting two worlds and leading to the exploration and colonization of the Western Hemisphere.

- British explorer James Cook undertook three epic voyages across the Pacific in the 18th century. He mapped uncharted territories, including the coastlines of Australia and New Zealand. His meticulous observations contributed to the understanding of ocean currents, geography, and indigenous cultures.

- Ibn Battuta, a Moroccan scholar, embarked on a remarkable journey in the 14th century. He traveled across Africa, Asia, and parts of Europe, covering over 75,000 miles. His travelog offers insights into diverse cultures and societies, providing a valuable historical record of the medieval world.

- Vasco da Gama, a Portuguese explorer, discovered a sea route to India in 1498. His voyage opened a profitable trade route, connecting Europe with the riches of the East. This route changed trade dynamics and reshaped global commerce.

- In 1969, American astronaut Neil Armstrong became the first person to set foot on the Moon. His iconic words, "That's one small step for [a] man, one giant leap for mankind," marked a historic achievement in space exploration and human endeavor.

o   Amelia Earhart, an American aviator, made groundbreaking strides in aviation during the early 20th century. She became the first woman to fly solo across the Atlantic Ocean and set numerous records. Her determination and courage continue to inspire aspiring pilots.

o   Scottish explorer David Livingstone ventured deep into the heart of Africa in the 19th century. His expeditions aimed to map uncharted territories and combat the slave trade. Livingstone's work led to increased knowledge of African geography and contributed to efforts to end slavery.

o   French explorer Jacques Cousteau is renowned for his underwater exploration and conservation efforts. He co-developed the Aqua-Lung, which revolutionized scuba diving. His documentaries showcased the beauty of marine life and raised awareness about the importance of ocean conservation.

o   Soviet cosmonaut Yuri Gagarin became the first human to orbit Earth in 1961. His spaceflight marked a major milestone in space exploration and demonstrated the potential for human space travel.

o   Mexican artist Frida Kahlo explored themes of identity and pain through her art. Her unique style and introspective paintings have made her an iconic figure in the art world, inspiring countless artists and admirers.

o Marco Polo, a Venetian merchant, embarked on an incredible journey to the distant lands of Asia in the 13th century. He traveled along the Silk Road, encountering vibrant cultures, exotic spices, and breathtaking landscapes. His written accounts of his travels introduced Europeans to the wonders of the East, from the opulence of Kublai Khan's court to the legendary city of Cathay. Polo's adventurous spirit and detailed descriptions inspired future explorers and ignited Europe's fascination with far-off lands.

o Fridtjof Nansen, a Norwegian explorer, made a remarkable contribution to polar exploration. In 1893, he embarked on a daring expedition to the Arctic Ocean aboard the ship Fram. Nansen intentionally allowed the ship to become trapped in ice, using it as a research station to study the Arctic's currents and ice movements. He even attempted to reach the North Pole on skis, leaving a trailblazing legacy in the realm of Arctic exploration. Nansen's innovative methods and determination paved the way for later expeditions in harsh polar environments.

o Roald Amundsen, a Norwegian explorer, achieved a historic milestone by becoming the first person to reach the South Pole. In 1911, he led an expedition that skillfully utilized dog sleds and meticulous planning. Amundsen's team reached the pole and returned safely, showcasing the significance of strategic planning, adaptability, and teamwork in conquering extreme environments. His success marked a pivotal moment in polar exploration and solidified his reputation as a pioneering figure.

o Dian Fossey, an American primatologist and conservationist, embarked on a groundbreaking journey to study and protect mountain gorillas in Rwanda. Her deep dedication led her to establish the Karisoke Research Center, where she conducted extensive research and advocated for the preservation of gorilla habitats. Fossey's passionate advocacy and efforts against poaching brought global attention to the plight of these magnificent creatures. Her story serves as a testament to the profound impact that one individual can have on the preservation of endangered species.

o Ernest Shackleton's ill-fated Antarctic expedition aboard the Endurance in 1914 is a story of resilience and leadership in the face of adversity. When the ship became trapped in ice, Shackleton and his crew faced daunting challenges, including surviving extreme cold and navigating treacherous ice floes. Despite the loss of their ship, Shackleton's extraordinary leadership ensured the survival of every crew member through a series of harrowing trials.

MYTHOLOGY

- o In Norse mythology, Thor, the god of thunder, wielded a powerful hammer called Mjölnir. It was said that only he could lift and wield this magical weapon, which could summon lightning and protect the gods from their enemies.

- o In Greek mythology, Medusa was a Gorgon with snakes for hair. Her gaze was so powerful that anyone who looked at her turned to stone. The hero Perseus managed to defeat her by using a reflective shield to avoid direct eye contact.

- o According to Egyptian mythology, the god Ra sailed across the sky in a boat called the "Barque of Ra" during the day and journeyed through the underworld at night. This symbolized the cycle of the sun rising and setting.

- o In Hindu mythology, the gods and demons worked together to churn the ocean to obtain the elixir of immortality. This epic event, known as the "Samudra Manthan," brought forth various treasures and divine beings, including the goddess Lakshmi.

- o Dragons hold a special place in Chinese mythology as symbols of power and prosperity. Unlike Western dragons, Chinese dragons are often depicted as benevolent and associated with water, bringing rain and good fortune.

- o In Japanese mythology, the kitsune is a fox spirit with shape-shifting abilities. It's believed to possess great intelligence and magical powers. Kitsune often serve as messengers, guardians, or tricksters in folktales.

- The Popol Vuh is an ancient Mayan sacred text that recounts the creation of the world and the adventures of the Hero Twins in the underworld. It provides insights into Mayan beliefs, cosmology, and cultural values.

- Quetzalcoatl, a prominent deity in Aztec mythology, was often depicted as a feathered serpent. He was associated with creation, learning, and culture. Quetzalcoatl's return was predicted to bring about significant changes.

- In Hawaiian mythology, Pele is the goddess of fire, lightning, wind, and volcanoes. She is believed to reside in the active Kilauea volcano and is both revered and feared as a powerful and unpredictable deity.

- Anansi is a prominent figure in African mythology, particularly among the Akan people of Ghana. Often depicted as a spider, Anansi is a trickster character known for his cleverness and ability to outwit larger and stronger foes

- According to Roman mythology, the city of Rome was founded by twin brothers Romulus and Remus, who were raised by a she-wolf. Romulus later became the first king of Rome, and the story of their origins is a central part of Roman history.

- In Inuit mythology, Sedna is the sea goddess and ruler of the underworld. She is associated with marine life and is believed to control the availability of sea animals for hunting. The story of Sedna explains the relationship between humans and the sea.

o   In Maori mythology of New Zealand, Tāne Mahuta is the god
    of forests and birds. He is credited with creating the first
    woman, Hineahuone, from clay. Tāne Mahuta is also known
    for separating his parents, the earth and sky, to bring light
    to the world.

o   In various Native American cultures, the coyote is a
    trickster figure who plays mischievous and often humorous
    roles in myths and stories. The coyote's antics often teach
    important lessons and explain the natural world.

o   In addition to gods, the Greeks believed in mythical
    creatures such as centaurs (half human, half horse) and
    Cyclopes (monsters with only one eye). These would often
    show up in mythology too.

o   Hanuman is a beloved figure in Hindu mythology and the
    central character in the epic Ramayana. He is a devoted
    disciple of Lord Rama and is known for his strength,
    courage, and loyalty. Hanuman is often depicted as a monkey
    deity.

o   Amaterasu is the sun goddess in Japanese mythology and a
    central figure in Shinto religion. It is believed that she
    emerged from a cave, bringing light back to the world after
    hiding in anger. Her story symbolizes the cycle of day and
    night.

o   Yggdrasil, the World Tree, is a significant symbol in Norse
    mythology. It is an immense tree that connects the nine
    realms of the Norse cosmology. Yggdrasil's branches extend
    over different worlds, and its roots reach into the realm of
    the dead.

- In some African myths, Anansi is not only a cunning spider but also the Sky God responsible for bringing rain and crops to the people. Anansi's role as a deity emphasizes the importance of nature and agriculture in African societies.

- In Polynesian mythology, Maui is a heroic figure known for his various exploits, such as slowing down the sun, fishing up islands, and even trying to achieve immortality. Maui's adventures are often used to explain natural phenomena and cultural practices.

KINGS AND QUEENS

- Kings and queens often have elaborate titles that reflect their status. For instance, Cleopatra VII of Egypt's full title was "Cleopatra Thea Philopator Philadelphus," emphasizing her divine and familial connections.

- In ancient Egypt, both kings and queens wore striking eye makeup called kohl, not just for aesthetics but also for its believed protective and medicinal properties.

- Queen Elizabeth I of England was not only a ruler but also a skilled musician and linguist. She was fluent in multiple languages, including Latin and French.

- King Louis XIV of France maintained a private menagerie that included exotic animals like lions, elephants, and giraffes. Visitors would marvel at these creatures as a display of royal wealth and power.

- Elizabeth II is the first British monarch to have a televised coronation and a televised Christmas address. She sent her first email from an army base in 1976, and sent the first royal tweet in 2014.

- Queen Teuta of Illyria, an ancient kingdom in the western Balkans, was known as a pirate queen. She led naval expeditions and raids, challenging Roman and Greek influence in the region.

- Tutankhamun, also known as King Tut, ascended the throne of Egypt at the age of nine. His reign was short but left behind a trove of treasures in his burial chamber.

o Queen Emma of Normandy, who lived during the 11th century, was known as a skilled diplomat and strategist. She played a pivotal role in the succession of English kings, earning her the nickname "Swan-Knight Queen."

o King Ludwig II of Bavaria, often referred to as the "Mad King," had a fascination with fairy tales and castles. He built the fantastical Neuschwanstein Castle, which served as inspiration for Disney's Sleeping Beauty Castle.

o King Tutankhamun's gold death mask is one of the most iconic artifacts from ancient Egypt. It was placed over the mummy's head and shoulders, believed to protect and guide the pharaoh's spirit.

o Queen Isabella I of Castile, who sponsored Christopher Columbus's voyage to the Americas, was said to be a skilled chess player. She even played against grandmasters of her time.

o Queen Boudica of the Iceni tribe in ancient Britain led a rebellion against Roman rule in the 1st century. Her fierce leadership and determination left an indelible mark on history.

o King Louis XVI of France was known for his elaborate fashion sense. He favored luxurious fabrics and intricate clothing, setting trends that influenced European fashion.

o The bust of Queen Nefertiti from ancient Egypt is one of the most famous and recognizable artifacts. Her exquisite beauty and regal expression have made her an enduring symbol of ancient royalty.

o   The discovery of King Tutankhamun's tomb in the 1920s was accompanied by stories of a "curse." Though not scientifically proven, the legend added to the intrigue surrounding the young pharaoh.

o   Empress Elisabeth of Austria, known as Sisi, was a passionate equestrian. She had a deep bond with her horses and often spent time riding and caring for them.

o   Cleopatra Queen of Egypt during 50 to 30 B.C. She came into power at 12 years old and married two of her brothers during her reign. It sounds crazy today, but this was fairly common practice back then!

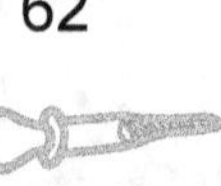

He
SO2
SCIENCE
Math
Cost

INVENTIONS AND INVENTORS

- Thomas Edison didn't actually invent the lightbulb. While it's true that he got a patent for the invention back in 1880, the real credit goes to Warren de la Rue, a British astronomer, and chemist who created the first bulb forty years earlier.

- The first camera was so big that it had to be carried on a wagon.

- The printing press, invented by Johannes Gutenberg, revolutionized the spread of knowledge in the 15th century.

- The telephone, patented by Alexander Graham Bell, changed communication by allowing voices to be transmitted over long distances.

- NASA engineer Lonnie G. Johnson invented the Super Soaker water gun by accident while testing a new type of heat pump. The pump's high-pressure stream of water gave him the idea for a powerful water toy.

- Dr. John Harvey Kellogg accidentally invented corn flakes in the late 19th century. He left boiled wheat sitting out and it became stale. When he rolled it out and baked it, it turned into flakes.

- French author Jules Verne's science fiction writings predicted several technological advances, including submarines, space travel, and lunar modules. His imagination foreshadowed real-life innovations.

- Henry Ford experimented with using potatoes to create plastic car parts in the 1940s. Due to wartime material shortages, he explored alternative materials, leading to the invention of soy-based plastic as well.

- Leonardo da Vinci designed a flying machine resembling a modern-day helicopter in the 15th century. While he never built a functional model, his sketches demonstrated his visionary thinking.

- Edwin Land, the founder of Polaroid Corporation, invented instant photography after his daughter questioned why she couldn't see a photograph immediately after it was taken.

- The ancient Greeks used a water clock called a "clepsydra" as an early form of an alarm clock. It worked by gradually filling a container with water, which would then make a noise when it reached a certain level.

- The microwave oven was accidentally invented by Percy Spencer, an engineer working for Raytheon, in 1945. He noticed that a candy bar in his pocket had melted while standing in front of a magnetron, a device that produces microwaves.

- Swiss engineer George de Mestral was inspired to invent Velcro after observing how burrs stuck to his dog's fur during a walk. He realized the potential for creating a fastening system based on this concept.

- Spencer Silver, a chemist at 3M, created a weak adhesive in 1968 that was later used by a colleague, Art Fry, to develop the iconic Post-it Notes in 1980.

- King C. Gillette introduced the safety razor with disposable blades in 1903. This innovation revolutionized shaving and laid the foundation for modern razor designs.

- The first artificial heart successfully implanted in a human was created by Dr. Robert Jarvik in 1982. The device, known as the Jarvik-7, kept the patient alive for 112 days while awaiting a heart transplant.

o   John W. Hetrick received a patent for the airbag in 1953. His initial concept was inspired by the safety cushions used to catch pilots who ejected from planes.

o   Theodore Maiman built the first functional laser in 1960 using a synthetic ruby crystal. This invention paved the way for numerous applications of laser technology, from medical procedures to communication.

o   The ballpoint pen was invented by Laszlo Biro, a Hungarian-Argentinian journalist, in 1938. He developed the pen as a way to create a more reliable writing instrument.

o   The precursor to the modern internet was ARPANET, a project initiated by the United States Department of Defense in the 1960s. It was designed to facilitate communication between research institutions and military sites.

o   James Watson and Francis Crick, along with Rosalind Franklin and Maurice Wilkins, discovered the structure of DNA in 1953. This groundbreaking work unlocked the secrets of genetics and laid the foundation for modern biotechnology.

o   Thomas Edison is known for inventing the practical incandescent lightbulb in 1879. He developed a carbon-filament bulb that could burn for over 40 hours.

o   Bubble wrap was initially designed as textured wallpaper. Its inventors, Alfred Fielding and Marc Chavannes, quickly realized its potential as a packing material when they noticed the satisfying sound it made when popped.

- Isaac de Rivaz, a Swiss engineer, created a hydrogen-powered vehicle in 1807. It used hydrogen gas to power an internal combustion engine, making it one of the earliest attempts at a fuel-efficient automobile.

- The first roller coaster was built in Russia in the 17th century. It was a large ice slide constructed for the amusement of Russian royalty during the winter.

PHYSICS AND CHEMISTRY

- The light bulb, developed by Thomas Edison, brought artificial light to homes and businesses.

- Carbon, a vital element for life, comes in different forms such as diamonds, graphite, and even in our own bodies.

- Mercury is the only metal that is liquid at room temperature.

- The element helium was first discovered in the Sun before being found on Earth.

- In the realm of quantum physics, particles can exist in multiple states simultaneously due to a phenomenon called superposition. This concept challenges our classical understanding of reality and is at the heart of quantum computing's potential.

- Quantum entanglement is a bizarre situation whereby particles become correlated in such a way that the state of one instantly affects the other, even if they're light-years apart. Einstein referred to this as "spooky action at a distance."

- The unification of electricity and magnetism, known as electromagnetism, paved the way for modern technological advancements. James Clerk Maxwell's equations elegantly described these forces, leading to innovations like radio waves and electric motors.

- Electromagnetic waves, from radio waves to gamma rays, are all around us, conveying information and energy without requiring a medium. This revolutionary understanding transformed communication and imaging technologies.

- Crystals are not only beautiful but also showcase the remarkable order in nature. Their repeating structure results in unique properties, such as piezoelectricity – generating electricity under mechanical stress.

- Alfred Nobel's invention of dynamite revolutionized construction and demolition. Ironically, his later contributions to science led to the establishment of the Nobel Prizes, distancing him from his destructive creation.

- Chemical bonds form when atoms share or transfer electrons. Understanding these bonds unlocks the secrets of molecular structures, from the double helix of DNA to the unique properties of water.

- Some colors in certain candies can disappear when you chew them! This is because the candies use a special kind of food coloring that's sensitive to pH levels in your mouth.

- Drop raisins into a glass of soda, and you'll see them "dance" up and down! This is because tiny bubbles of carbon dioxide stick to the raisins and make them float.

- Magnets have invisible "force fields" around them. You can use magnets to make objects move without touching them, like when you push two magnets together and feel them repel each other.

- You can make a rainbow in a glass of water by shining a flashlight through it. This happens because light bends when it passes through the water, just like a real rainbow in the sky.

- Pop Rocks candy pops and crackles in your mouth because they release tiny gas bubbles when they come into contact with your saliva.

o Mix baking soda and vinegar together, and you'll see a fizzy explosion! You can even add food coloring to make it a colorful eruption.

o Try placing a candy in water and watch its colors spread out! This is similar to how detectives analyze ink to figure out what it's made of.

o Some things float in water, while others sink. This is because of their density – how much stuff is packed into a certain space. An empty bottle floats, but if you fill it with water, it sinks!

o Ever wonder why you can hear sizzling sounds when you cook? It's because the heat makes the air around the food vibrate, and your ears catch those vibrations as sound waves.

o When you rub a balloon against your hair and it sticks, that's static electricity at work! The balloon becomes charged, and your hair has the opposite charge, so they stick together.

o Some things glow under certain lights, like a white T-shirt glowing in a dark room when you shine a blacklight on it. This is because of a special glow called fluorescence.

DISCOVERIES

- Alexander Fleming stumbled upon the world-changing antibiotic penicillin in 1928 when he noticed that a mold, Penicillium, had killed off bacteria in a petri dish he had forgotten to cover. This chance observation revolutionized medicine.

- Jocelyn Bell Burnell discovered the first radio pulsar in 1967. Initially, the rhythmic radio signals were so precise that they were jokingly labeled "Little Green Men." This serendipitous discovery expanded our understanding of celestial bodies.

- Arno Penzias and Robert Wilson accidentally detected the cosmic microwave background radiation, an afterglow of the Big Bang, while trying to isolate noise in a large radio telescope. Their findings provided crucial evidence for the Big Bang theory.

- Wilhelm Conrad Roentgen discovered X-rays in 1895 while experimenting with cathode rays. He noticed a mysterious glow on a nearby chemically coated screen, unveiling a new form of penetrating radiation.

- Swiss engineer George de Mestral invented Velcro in 1948 after examining burrs that clung to his dog's fur during a walk. He realized that the tiny hooks and loops of the burrs could be mimicked in a fastening material.

- The discovery of viruses, invisible to standard microscopes, required the development of the electron microscope. In 1939, German physicist Ernst Ruska's work on electron lenses paved the way for the first viral images.

- Otto Hahn and Fritz Strassmann, while trying to transmute uranium atoms, accidentally discovered nuclear fission in 1938. Their results baffled them until Lise Meitner and Otto Frisch explained that atoms were splitting.

- In 1974, a group of Chinese farmers discovered the incredible Terracotta Army while digging a well. The thousands of life-sized clay soldiers guarding the tomb of China's first emperor were a testament to ancient craftsmanship.

- In 1907, Bertram Boltwood discovered radioactive dating while studying the radioactive decay of uranium into lead. He realized that this process could be used to determine the age of rocks and minerals.

- In 1984, scientists discovered a meteorite in Antarctica that originated from Mars. The meteorite contained what appeared to be signs of past microbial life, sparking debates about the possibility of extraterrestrial life.

- Sir William Herschel accidentally discovered infrared radiation in 1800. While conducting experiments with a prism to measure the temperatures of different colors, he noticed an increase in temperature beyond the red end of the visible spectrum.

- Marie Curie's discovery of radium and polonium revolutionized our understanding of radioactivity. Her relentless work led to the term "radioactivity" itself and paved the way for groundbreaking research in nuclear physics.

- Dom Pérignon, a Benedictine monk, didn't set out to create champagne, but his meticulous observations and innovative techniques in winemaking inadvertently led to the effervescent delight we know today.

- In the 18th century, Swedish chemist Carl Wilhelm Scheele and English chemist Joseph Priestley independently discovered oxygen. Priestley referred to the gas as "dephlogisticated air," while Scheele called it "fire air."

- Henri Becquerel accidentally discovered radioactivity while studying the effects of sunlight on uranium salts. He found that even when shielded from light, the uranium emitted mysterious penetrating rays.

- In the early 20th century, British archaeologist Howard Carter discovered the immense stone circle of Stonehenge, but its origins and purpose remain subjects of intense speculation and research.

- German chemist Hennig Brand stumbled upon phosphorus in 1669 while trying to create the philosopher's stone. His quest led him to boil down urine, discovering the element's luminous properties.

- Rosalind Franklin's expertise in X-ray crystallography led to her capturing "Photo 51," an image that played a vital role in deciphering the structure of DNA. Her work, while uncredited at the time, was instrumental in the discovery of DNA's double helix.

- The first photographs of a live giant squid were captured in 2004. Researchers used a specialized camera to record these elusive deep-sea creatures over 2,000 feet underwater.

o   In 2006, the definition of a planet changed, resulting in the reclassification of Pluto as a "dwarf planet." This reevaluation sparked discussions about the criteria that define celestial bodies in our solar system.

o   Discovered in a shipwreck in 1901, the Antikythera Mechanism is an ancient Greek analog computer that could predict astronomical positions and eclipses. Its complexity surprised historians and revealed advanced ancient knowledge of the cosmos.

o   In the Namib Desert, mysterious circular patches of bare ground known as "fairy circles" were discovered. These patterns have sparked numerous theories, from termites' involvement to underground water dynamics.

o   Modern imaging techniques and research, including DNA analysis, have revealed fascinating insights into Pharaoh Tutankhamun's life and lineage, dispelling myths and uncovering his remarkable story.

o   The discovery of quantum entanglement revealed that particles can be connected in such a way that changes to one particle instantaneously affect another, regardless of distance. Albert Einstein famously referred to this as "spooky action at a distance."

o   Though yet to be directly detected, the existence of dark matter was inferred from its gravitational effects on galaxies. This elusive substance constitutes a significant portion of the universe's mass and energy content.

ANIMALS

MAMMALS

- Mammals are warm-blooded, which means they can regulate their body temperature. Whether it's a chilly winter day or a scorching summer afternoon, mammals stay cozy!

- Most mammals have fur or hair covering their bodies. This fur helps them stay warm, protects their skin, and can even be different colors and patterns.

- Mammal babies are born alive and are usually tiny compared to their parents. They grow and develop inside their mother's womb, just like you did!

- Mammals have a wide range of diets. Some are carnivores (meat-eaters), for example lions and tigers. Others are herbivores (plant-eaters), such as cows and deer. And some are omnivores (both meat and plant-eaters), like humans!

- Bats are the only mammals that can truly fly. They have special wings made of skin stretched over long finger bones. So, bats are like the sky's acrobats!

- Dolphins, whales, and porpoises are mammals that have evolved to live in the water. They breathe air, just like you, but they're experts at swimming and diving.

- The blue whale is the largest mammal on Earth! It's even bigger than the dinosaurs. Imagine a creature as heavy as 200 elephants swimming through the ocean!

- Elephants have incredible memories. They can remember places, other elephants, and even special events for many years. It's like they have their own elephant encyclopedia!

- Squirrels are quite the social animals. They communicate using chatters and tail flicks, and they even share their food with other squirrels in times of need.

- Primates, like monkeys and apes, are mammals that are most similar to humans. They have hands with five fingers (just like us!), and they can do some pretty clever things.

- Dolphins use a series of clicks, whistles, and body movements to talk to each other. They have their own underwater language!

- Dogs have an incredible sense of smell. It's estimated that a dog's nose is about 40 times more sensitive than a human's nose. That's why they're such great sniffers!

- Some mammals, like owls and bats, are nocturnal. This means they're most active at night. Their special adaptations help them navigate and find food in the dark.

- Monkeys are excellent climbers. With their strong arms and legs, they can swing from trees and leap between branches. They're nature's acrobats!

- Did you know that some mammals, like dolphins and certain bats, use echolocation to find their way around? They make sounds that bounce off objects and return as echoes, helping them "see" their surroundings.

INSECTS

- Monarch butterflies migrate up to 3,000 miles from North America to Mexico to escape the cold. Wildebeests in Africa travel hundreds of miles during the Great Migration, braving crocodile-filled rivers. These journeys showcase nature's incredible drive for survival.

- The bombardier beetle has an explosive defense mechanism. When threatened, it shoots out a hot and stinky chemical spray, deterring predators with a pungent surprise!

- Animals like the bowerbird and pufferfish create impressive homes. Bowerbirds craft intricate nests adorned with colorful objects to attract mates. Pufferfish create mesmerizing underwater patterns to mark their territory and attract a partner.

- Flower mantises resemble blossoms to ambush unsuspecting prey. These masters of mimicry use deception as a survival strategy.

- Ants are tiny but mighty! Some ant colonies can have millions of worker ants, all working together like a well-organized army to gather food, build nests, and defend their territory.

- Fleas are incredible jumpers. They can leap up to 350 times their body length, which is like a person jumping the length of a football field in one jump!

- The termite might look small, but its architectural prowess is immense. Termites build towering mounds that can be taller than a human. These mounds have complex air conditioning systems that keep the colony cool in hot weather.

- Crickets are famous for their nighttime serenades, but did you know that they make these sounds by rubbing their wings together? It's like they're playing a mini violin!

- Fireflies, or lightning bugs, light up the night with their magical glows. They use their light to communicate with each other, whether it's to find a mate or warn predators to stay away.

- Stick insects have a unique way of staying hidden. They look just like twigs or leaves, which helps them blend in perfectly with their surroundings. It's nature's best disguise!

- Bees are remarkable builders. Honeybees construct intricate hexagon-shaped cells out of wax to store honey and raise their young. It's like they're creating their own honeycomb city.

- Dragonflies have enormous eyes that cover almost their entire head. These eyes have thousands of tiny lenses, giving them incredible vision to spot prey and predators.

- Spider silk is stronger than steel of the same thickness. Some spiders use their silk to create intricate webs that are like nature's engineering marvels, designed to catch food on the fly.

- The water strider is like a superhero of the insect world. It can "walk" on the surface of water without sinking, thanks to tiny hairs that repel water and create air pockets.

- The Hercules beetle has the strongest bite of any animal. It can lift objects up to 850 times its body weight using its powerful jaws. That's equivalent to a person lifting a school bus!

o Honeybees have an incredible way of telling their hive-mates where to find food. They perform a special dance called the "waggle dance" to communicate the direction and distance of nectar sources.

o A bee's wings beat 190 times a second, that's 11,400 times a minute.

o One dung beetle can drag 1,141 times its weight - that's like a human pulling six double-decker buses!

o When you're in a hot country, you can sometimes hear a strange noise...It might be crickets.
   The chirping noise crickets make is caused when they rub their wing across each other.
   It's called stridulation. Grasshoppers do it too!

o Grasshoppers existed before dinosaurs! Wow! Dinosaurs roamed the Earth around 66 million years ago. However, it is believed that the grasshopper's ancient ancestors lived before dinosaurs even roamed the Earth. Scientists found this out because of fossils that they found. Grasshoppers could be around 300 million years old!

REPTILES AND AMPHIBIANS

- Turtles and tortoises have been around for a very long time - even before dinosaurs! They're like living fossils, carrying the secrets of Earth's ancient past.

- Snakes have a superpower - they can "see" heat! Some snakes have special sensors called heat pits that allow them to detect warm-blooded animals, even in the dark.

- Chameleons are the ultimate color-changing artists. They change colors to communicate with other chameleons, regulate their body temperature, and even show their emotions.

- Some lizards can regrow their tails if they lose them! It's like having a built-in superhero power to escape from predators.

- Amphibians, such as frogs and salamanders, can live both in water and on land. They start as tadpoles with gills for breathing underwater, and then transform into adults with lungs.

- Frogs are amazing singers. Different species have unique calls that they use to find mates and establish their territory. It's like a nighttime orchestra in wetlands!

- Some salamanders have a secret power - they can regrow entire limbs! If a predator grabs their tail, they can simply shed it and grow a new one later.

- Toads have a defense mechanism called "bufotoxin." If threatened, they puff up their bodies to appear larger and secrete a toxic substance that can deter predators.

- The axolotl is like a real-life magical creature. It retains its juvenile features even as it grows into adulthood, a process called neoteny. Plus, it can regenerate its limbs, spinal cord, and even parts of its heart and brain!

- Many amphibians have slimy skin that helps them stay moist and breathe through their skin. It's like having built-in sunscreen and a breathing system all in one.

- Male frogs can serenade females with special calls to attract them for mating. Each species has its own unique song, making it a symphony of love songs in the frog world.

- The Chinese giant salamander is the largest amphibian in the world. It can grow up to six feet long, making it a true giant of the amphibian realm.

- Crocodiles have been on Earth for over 200 million years, surviving through the age of dinosaurs and into our modern times. They're like living time travelers!

- Geckos have an amazing ability to climb walls and even walk upside down on ceilings. They use special toe pads covered in microscopic hairs that create a strong adhesive force.

- Alligators are incredible engineers of their environment. They create "gator holes" by digging out depressions in the ground that fill with water during the rainy season, providing homes for other animals during dry times.

- Sea turtles are true globetrotters. Some species of sea turtles migrate thousands of miles between their nesting and feeding areas, navigating by using Earth's magnetic field.

- Some frogs have a slimy secret weapon. Their skin can secrete toxins that help protect them from predators. But don't worry, these toxins won't harm you if you touch them gently!

- Glass frogs have eggs that are almost see-through! This allows scientists to observe the developing embryos inside the eggs without even cracking them open.

- Some frogs have the ability to survive freezing temperatures. They enter a state of suspended animation, where their bodies slow down so much that they seem almost lifeless, until they thaw out when it gets warmer.

- Male frogs in some species create beautiful "nuptial pads" on their thumbs during mating season. These pads help them grip onto their mates while they perform complex acrobatic mating dances.

- Chameleons have lightning-fast tongues that can shoot out to catch insects in a fraction of a second. Their tongues are longer than their whole body and can stretch up to twice their body length!

- Some frogs communicate with each other through a special dance called "foot-flagging." They lift and wave their brightly colored feet to signal their presence to potential mates.

BIRDS

- The wandering albatross has one of the largest wingspans of any bird, reaching up to 11 feet (3.4 meters)! This allows them to glide effortlessly for miles without flapping their wings.

- The dawn chorus is a beautiful phenomenon where many birds sing together at sunrise. Each species has its own unique song, and it's like a musical orchestra welcoming the new day.

- Male peacocks display their vibrant tail feathers, called "eyespots," to attract females. Interestingly, those eyespots look like the eyes of a larger predator, which can confuse potential threats.

- The peregrine falcon is the fastest bird in the world, reaching speeds of over 240 mph (386 km/h) when diving to catch prey. This makes it an incredible aerial predator.

- The superb lyrebird of Australia is a fantastic mimic. It can imitate a wide range of sounds it hears, including chainsaws, camera shutters, and other bird calls.

- The bee hummingbird, found in Cuba and Isla de la Juventud, is the smallest bird in the world, measuring just around 2 inches (5 cm) long. Despite its small size, it's an excellent flier.

- The European robin is known for its red breast and cheerful song. But did you know they're also skilled at perching on a variety of objects, from branches to fence posts?

- Some parrots, like the African gray parrot, have an incredible ability to mimic human speech and sounds. They can even understand the meaning of some words!

- The ostrich lays the largest eggs of any bird. These enormous eggs are about the size of a cantaloupe and can weigh over 3 pounds (1.4 kg)!

- The Arctic tern holds the record for the longest migratory journey. It travels from the Arctic to the Antarctic and back each year, covering a distance of about 44,000 miles (71,000 km).

- Eagles have incredible vision, with some species able to spot a rabbit from more than two miles away! They also have two sets of color receptors, allowing them to see a broader spectrum of colors.

- The male bowerbird goes to great lengths to impress potential mates. They build elaborate bowers (structures made of twigs and decorated with colorful items) and perform intricate dances to showcase their creativity.

- Homing pigeons are excellent navigators. They can find their way back home from distances of hundreds of miles, even when released in unfamiliar locations.

- The birds-of-paradise, found in Papua New Guinea and nearby islands, are renowned for their mesmerizing courtship displays. Each species has its own unique dance routine to attract females.

- Owls can rotate their heads up to 270 degrees, thanks to their specialized neck structure. This allows them to scan their surroundings without moving their bodies.

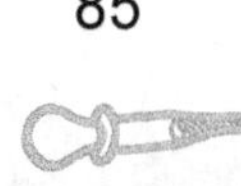

- The Atlantic puffin is an exceptional swimmer. It can dive as deep as 200 feet (60 meters) to catch fish, using its wings to "fly" underwater.

- Emperor penguins are known for their tight-knit communities in Antarctica. They huddle together to stay warm during harsh winters, taking turns to move to the center of the huddle for warmth.

- The Harris's hawk, found in North and South America, is known for its cooperative hunting behavior. They work together in small groups to catch prey, displaying an exceptional level of teamwork.

- Male weaverbirds construct intricate nests made of woven grass. These nests not only provide shelter but also play a role in attracting females for mating.

- The common kingfisher is a skilled fisher bird that can dive into water at high speeds to catch fish. Its streamlined body and specialized eyes help it spot prey even underwater.

- The bar-tailed godwit undertakes one of the longest non-stop migrations of any bird. It flies from Alaska to New Zealand without stopping, covering around 7,000 miles (11,000 km).

- New Caledonian crows are known for their tool-making abilities. They fashion tools from leaves, twigs, and other objects to extract insects and other food sources.

- The palm cockatoo of northern Australia is a unique drummer. Using a stick or seedpod, they rhythmically drum on tree branches to communicate with other cockatoos.

o The Australian brush-turkey builds large mounds out of leaves, twigs, and soil, which serve as incubators for their eggs. The heat generated by the mound's decomposition helps hatch the eggs.

o All birds have feathers and they are very useful for lots of different reasons. Feathers help birds to fly. They help to control the wind when flying through the air. They also keep birds warm in the winter!
Did you know that birds also use their feathers to show off?
A peacock does exactly this! A peacock will show all of his feathers to attract a mate.

o Birds are great communicators. Birds chirp and sing. They do this for lots of different reasons.One of the reasons is to attract a mate. Another reason is to warn other birds of danger. They also do it to scare off predators!

o Some birds, like the homing pigeons, are bred to find their way back home from long distances. They were used for thousands of years to carry messages.

o Birds have hollow bones which help them fly.

OCEAN LIFE

- Some ocean creatures emit radiant glows through biofluorescence. Coral reefs transform into colorful spectacles as fish radiate vibrant colors. It's a mesmerizing display hidden beneath the waves.

- Cleaner fish offer a cleaning service to larger fish, removing parasites and gaining a meal in return. Clownfish live safely within sea anemones, which shield them from predators. These partnerships demonstrate nature's intricate balance.

- Microorganisms like diatoms sculpt intricate shells, and tardigrades survive extreme conditions. These microscopic life forms play vital roles in ecosystems and hold the secrets to resilience.

- Some creatures in the ocean, like the firefly squid, produce bioluminescent light. This natural light helps them attract prey, communicate, and even confuse predators.

- The blue whale, the largest animal on Earth, can grow to be over 100 feet long and weigh as much as 200 tons. Its heart alone can be as big as a small car!

- The mimic octopus is a master of disguise. It can change its color, texture, and shape to mimic other marine animals, such as lionfish, flatfish, and even sea snakes.

- The anglerfish, found in the deep ocean, has a unique way of attracting prey. A bioluminescent lure dangles in front of its mouth, tempting unsuspecting fish into its grasp.

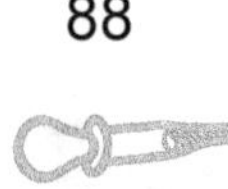

- Jellyfish have been drifting through the oceans for over 500 million years, making them one of the oldest living creatures on Earth. They have simple bodies composed mainly of water.

- Coral reefs are the largest living structures on the planet, built by tiny coral animals called polyps over thousands of years. These reefs are home to an incredible diversity of marine life.

- Octopuses are incredibly intelligent creatures. They can solve puzzles, open jars, and even use tools to catch their prey. Some species can change the color and texture of their skin to blend into their surroundings.

- The leatherback sea turtle holds the record for the longest migratory route of any marine creature. They travel thousands of miles between their nesting and feeding grounds.

- Schools of fish, like sardines and herring, move together in coordinated patterns to confuse predators and find food. This behavior is called "shoaling."

- Archerfish have a unique way of catching insects. They shoot water droplets from their mouths to knock insects off leaves and into the water, where they become a tasty meal.

- The deep-sea gulper eel has a mouth that can expand to allow it to swallow prey larger than its own body size. This adaptation helps it survive in the dark depths.

- The sailfish is one of the fastest fish in the ocean, reaching speeds of up to 68 miles per hour (110 km/h). They use their large dorsal fin, resembling a sail, to help them move swiftly.

DINOSAURS

o Dinosaurs were a diverse group of animals that roamed the Earth for millions of years. They came in all shapes and sizes, from tiny bird-like creatures to gigantic, long-necked sauropods.

o Dinosaurs lived during the Mesozoic Era, which is divided into three periods: the Triassic, Jurassic, and Cretaceous. Each period had its own unique set of dinosaurs.

o Sauropods, like the Brachiosaurus and Apatosaurus, had incredibly long necks and tails. They were some of the largest land animals ever, and their immense size helped them reach vegetation high up in trees.

o The Compsognathus was a small dinosaur about the size of a chicken. Despite its size, it was a swift and agile predator that hunted insects and small animals.

o Ankylosaurs were heavily armored dinosaurs with bony plates and spikes on their backs. They used their armored body as protection against predators.

o The Carnotaurus had short arms, but it made up for it with sharp teeth and a horned skull. Its name means "meat-eating bull," reflecting its fearsome appearance.

o Spinosaurus is known for its sail-like structure on its back and a long snout filled with sharp teeth. It's believed that Spinosaurus may have spent a lot of time in water, hunting fish.

- The Mesozoic Era came to an end with a mass extinction event around 65 million years ago. This event wiped out most dinosaurs, making way for the rise of mammals and other new life forms.

- Dinosaur fossils have been found on every single continent! This means they lived everywhere!

- The biggest dinosaur bone that also holds the largest fossil record ever found was a backbone. It weighed over a ton!

- There was a dinosaur fossil that was found with both a Velociraptor and Protoceratops. They were attacking each other and scientists could see that in the fossil!

- Velociraptors were much smaller than portrayed in movies, closer to the size of a turkey.

- The longest dinosaur ever discovered is the Argentinosaurus, which could reach up to 100 feet in length.

- The word "dinosaur" comes from the Greek words "deinos" and "sauros," which together mean "terrible lizard."

- The smallest known dinosaur is the Microraptor, which was only about 2 feet (0.6 meters) long.

- Some dinosaurs had feathers, which suggests that they might have looked more like birds than reptiles.

- The Tyrannosaurus rex had tiny, two-fingered arms, but they were strong and could hold prey.

- Triceratops had a massive frill at the back of its head, which scientists believe might have been used for display or defense.

- The Stegosaurus had plates along its back that were likely used for regulating body temperature.

- The Brachiosaurus, with its long neck, was able to feed on vegetation high in trees.

- The Velociraptor had a sharp, sickle-shaped claw on its foot that it likely used for hunting.

- The Pterosaur, often mistaken for a dinosaur, was actually a flying reptile.

- The Ankylosaurus had armor-like plates and a clubbed tail for protection.

- Some dinosaurs, like the Spinosaurus, were adapted for both land and water.

- The Parasaurolophus had a long, curved crest on its head that might have been used for communication.

- The Deinonychus is believed to be closely related to birds and is considered one of the more intelligent dinosaurs.

- The Brachiosaurus had nostrils on top of its head, allowing it to breathe while partially submerged in water.

- Some dinosaurs, like the Iguanodon, had a thumb spike that might have been used for defense.

- The largest land predator ever was Spinosaurus, even bigger than T. rex.

- Archeopteryx is considered a "transitional fossil" between dinosaurs and modern birds.

- Stegosaurus had a tiny brain, about the size of a walnut, relative to its body size.

- Some dinosaurs, like the Troodon, had larger brains relative to their body size and were likely more intelligent.

- Some dinosaurs had hollow bones, making them lighter and potentially aiding in flight.

- Dinosaurs laid eggs, and some parents may have cared for their nests.

- Some fossils show signs of injuries or diseases that the dinosaurs suffered from.

- The Velociraptor likely had feathers and might have been more bird-like in appearance.

- The Allosaurus had serrated teeth that helped it tear through flesh.

- Many dinosaurs had specialized teeth for different types of eating, like grinding or tearing.

- Sauropods like the Diplodocus had long necks but swallowed stones to aid in digestion.

- The T. rex was one of the last known dinosaurs to exist before the mass extinction event.

- The Triceratops' frill could grow to be over 6 feet (1.8 meters) wide.

- The Edmontosaurus had hundreds of teeth in its mouth to help it grind through plant material.

- The Troodon had large eyes relative to its body size, suggesting it might have been nocturnal.

- The Anzu wyliei, also known as the "chicken from hell," was a strange-looking dinosaur with a bird-like beak.

- Some dinosaurs, like the Compsognathus, were about the size of a chicken.

- The Segnosaurus had a beak and leaf-shaped teeth, suggesting a unique diet.

- The Deinocheirus had long arms with massive claws, which were initially discovered before the rest of the skeleton.

- The Hesperornis was a flightless bird-like dinosaur that lived underwater.

- The Corythosaurus had a hollow crest on its head, which might have been used for producing sounds.

- The Tsintaosaurus had a crest that resembled a horse's saddle.

- The Velociraptor's curved, sickle-shaped claw on its foot was used for hunting and climbing.

- The Quetzalcoatlus was one of the largest flying animals ever, with a wingspan of around 36 feet (11 meters).

- The Therizinosaurus had the longest claws of any known dinosaur, reaching up to 3 feet (1 meter) in length.

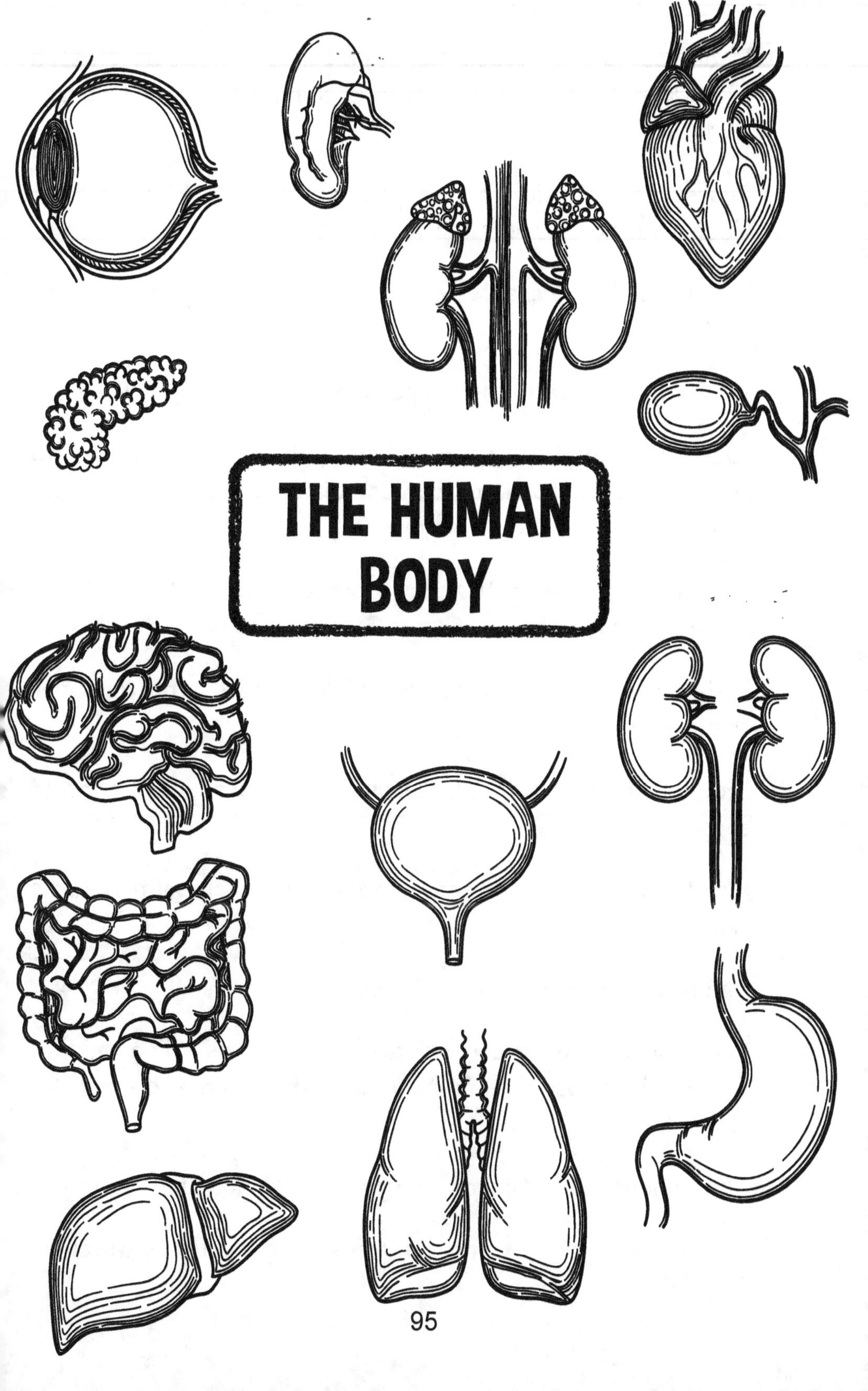
THE HUMAN
BODY

- If all your blood vessels were unwound, they would stretch 100,000 miles long! This means it could stretch around the earth many times.

- Tears are essential to help you see clearly. When you get older, you produce less tears.

- The human heart creates enough pressure to squirt blood 30 feet!

- You blink over 10,000 times per day or 12 times per minute.

- Out of all of the senses, smell is most closely linked to memory – which explains why certain smells bring back vivid memories!

- Babies take 40 breaths per minute. Adults take 12 to 16 breaths per minute.

- Bodies give off a tiny amount of light that's too weak for the eye to see.

- The human body contains enough fat to produce 7 bars of soap!

- Blood is blue until it reaches oxygen, at which point it turns red!

- The human brain is about 80% water.

- Your fingernails grow at different rates. The middle fingernail grows the fastest and the thumb grows the slowest.

- Throughout your lifetime, you grow 590 miles of hair.

- The human brain is more active sleeping than it is watching TV!

o A human will eat approximately 35 tons of food over the course of his or her lifetime.

o You are taller in the morning than you are at night.

o It would take about 100,000 mosquitoes sucking your blood to drain it out completely.

o A baby is born with 300 bones but only 206 bones as an adult because some of them fuse together.

o People with blue eyes tend to be more sensitive to bright light than people who have other eye colors!

o Your heart beats about 115,000 every day.

o The human body is made up of about 37 trillion cells.

o The human eye comprises about 2 million working parts.

o The human brain will triple its size in the first year of life.

o The brain is actually not capable of multitasking. While we may think we're doing two things at the same time, we're actually just quickly switching back and forth between different tasks.

o Women's hearts beat faster than men's.

o Each person's fingerprint is entirely unique, making it an essential tool in forensic science and identification.

o Your skin is your body's largest organ and serves as a barrier against harmful substances while regulating body temperature.

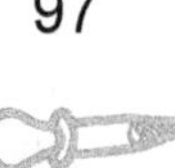

- The masseter muscle in your jaw is one of the strongest muscles in your body, capable of exerting tremendous force while chewing.

- The gut contains an intricate network of neurons, often referred to as the "second brain," influencing mood and well-being.

- Your bones are constantly being replaced in a process called remodeling, with most of your skeleton being renewed every 10 years.

- Your eyes can distinguish about 10 million different colors, allowing you to perceive a vivid and rich visual world.

- The brain generates around 20 watts of electrical power when awake, enough to light a dim light bulb.

- Tendons connect muscles to bones and are incredibly strong. In fact, they can bear loads of over 8,000 pounds!

- Your mouth is home to millions of bacteria, more than the entire population of people on Earth.

- Tooth enamel is the hardest substance in your body and cannot repair itself once damaged.

- When you sneeze, the air can rush out of your nose at speeds of up to 100 miles per hour!

- Your kidneys filter around 200 quarts of blood daily to remove waste products and excess fluids.

- There are three tiny bones in your ear called the hammer, anvil, and stirrup, which transmit sound vibrations to your inner ear.

FOOD

o Spicy foods trigger a release of endorphins in your brain, creating a natural "spice high" that's responsible for the addictive thrill of heat.

o Archaeologists have found pots of honey in ancient Egyptian tombs that are over 3,000 years old and still perfectly edible.

o Certain species of mushrooms can conduct electricity. In fact, the "electric" properties of some mushrooms were used in ancient times to create simple batteries.

o Popcorn was enjoyed by ancient civilizations long before the invention of microwaves. Prehistoric popcorn kernels have been found in archaeological sites in Peru.

o Edible gold leaf is used in some extravagant dishes and desserts around the world. It's safe to eat and adds a touch of luxury to culinary creations.

o Bananas contain a small amount of naturally occurring radioactivity due to the presence of potassium-40 isotopes.

o The record for eating the most Big Macs in one lifetime is held by a man who consumed over 30,000 of them!

o In 1947, a molasses tank exploded in Boston, resulting in a "chocolate rain" that flooded streets with over two million gallons of the sticky substance.

o Sushi chefs often study for years to perfect their craft. The right rice consistency, fish freshness, and knife skills are crucial to creating the perfect sushi.

o Imagine if ice cream could be made using liquid nitrogen! In some places, that's a reality. Liquid nitrogen is super cold, and when it's added to ice cream ingredients, it freezes them instantly, creating a creamy treat right before your eyes. This special method is used to make ultra-smooth and extra-frosty ice cream.

o Have you ever heard of a fizzy drink called kombucha? It's made by fermenting sweet tea with a special mix of bacteria and yeast. During fermentation, the yeast produces bubbles, giving the drink its fizzy kick. Plus, kombucha is filled with probiotics, which are tiny helpers that can be good for your tummy!

o The magical journey from cacao beans to chocolate bars is quite a process! Cacao beans are harvested, fermented, dried, roasted, and ground into a paste called cocoa mass. Then comes the fun part: adding sugar and milk, mixing, and letting it all set. Finally, you get to enjoy the delicious treat we all love – chocolate!

o Sushi is a Japanese dish that's both tasty and artistic. Did you know that the word "sushi" doesn't mean "raw fish"? It actually refers to the vinegared rice used in the dish. Sushi can be made with all sorts of ingredients, like cooked or raw fish, vegetables, and even fruits. It's like a tiny masterpiece you can eat!

o It takes about 50 licks to finish just one scoop of ice cream.

o Hawaiian pizza was actually invented in Canada.

o Did you know you can buy pyramid shaped watermelons in Japan!

o   The world's longest French fry is 34-inches long.

o   The earliest menu dates back to the mid-1700s. They first popped up in Europe around then to accommodate high-class residents during dinner parties.

o   Chocolate dates back to ancient Mesoamerican civilizations like the Mayans and Aztecs, who consumed it as a bitter beverage rather than the sweet treat we know today.

o   Ice cream cones were invented at the 1904 World's Fair in St. Louis when an ice cream vendor ran out of cups. He teamed up with a waffle vendor, and the ice cream cone was born!

o   Nutella, the beloved hazelnut spread, was created during World War II when cocoa was in short supply. A pastry maker mixed hazelnuts into chocolate to extend the supply.

o   In the past, lobsters were considered a poor man's food and were fed to prisoners and servants. It wasn't until the mid-19th century that they gained their upscale reputation.

o   Around the world, you can find ice cream flavors like squid ink, garlic, wasabi, and even curry. People's tastes for frozen treats vary widely!

o   Some types of cheese, like Mimolette, are intentionally infested with tiny cheese mites that help develop their distinct flavors and textures.

o   Most wasabi served in restaurants isn't real wasabi but a mixture of horseradish, mustard, and green food coloring. Authentic wasabi is rare and expensive.

PLANTS

TREES

- Trees share information through a "Wood Wide Web" - a network of fungi and roots. They exchange nutrients, alerts about threats, and resources. This communication system helps trees support each other.

- Some of the oldest living organisms on Earth are trees. For example, the bristlecone pine trees found in California's White Mountains can live for over 5,000 years!

- Coastal redwood trees are some of the tallest trees on the planet and can grow over 300 feet (91 meters) tall. They're so tall that they can create their own microclimates by pulling moisture from coastal fog.

- Trees have rings inside their trunks that can reveal a lot about their history. Each ring represents a year of growth and can provide information about climate conditions, forest fires, and even insect infestations.

- Maple trees produce sap that can be boiled down to make delicious maple syrup. It takes about 40 liters of sap to make just one liter of syrup!

- Trees can act as natural lightning rods. The moisture in their trunks can conduct electricity from lightning strikes safely into the ground, reducing the risk of fires.

- Trees play a crucial role in producing oxygen. A single mature tree can produce enough oxygen for two people to breathe in a year.

- The practice of hugging trees, known as "tree hugging," is not only a symbol of environmentalism but also has scientific benefits. Studies show that spending time around trees can reduce stress and improve overall well-being.

- The bark of different tree species can have unique patterns and textures. Some trees, like the cork oak, have bark that can be harvested without harming the tree itself.

- The ginkgo tree is often referred to as a "living fossil" because it has remained relatively unchanged for millions of years. Its distinctive fan-shaped leaves can be found in fossils dating back to the time of dinosaurs.

- Trees help improve air quality by absorbing carbon dioxide and releasing oxygen during photosynthesis. They also filter out pollutants from the air, making urban areas healthier places to live.

- Trees need to drink a lot of water! A large oak tree can consume 100 gallons of water daily, while a giant sequoia can drink up to 500 gallons daily.

- Trees provide homes and shelter for countless animals, from birds nesting in their branches to insects living in their bark. They are essential for maintaining biodiversity.

- The vibrant colors of autumn leaves are caused by pigments in the leaves, including chlorophyll (green), carotenoids (yellow and orange), and anthocyanins (red and purple).

FLOWERS

- Dandelion seeds float in the wind, using air travel to find new homes. Bright flowers lure pollinators, like bees and butterflies, to aid in spreading their pollen. Fig trees rely on wasps to pollinate them while ensuring the wasps a safe haven.

- In the Victorian era, flowers were often used to convey emotions and messages, known as the "language of flowers." Each flower had a specific meaning, allowing people to communicate sentiments without words.

- The Rafflesia arnoldii holds the title for the world's largest flower. Found in Southeast Asia, it can reach up to 3 feet (91 centimeters) in diameter and emits a foul odor to attract pollinators.

- Some flowers are edible and used in cooking. Examples include nasturtiums, which have a peppery flavor and are often added to salads, and roses, which can be used to make rose water and jams.

- The Titan arum, also known as the "corpse flower," is infamous for its strong odor resembling a rotting corpse. It's one of the largest and rarest flowers in the world.

- Sunflowers have a unique behavior known as heliotropism, where they turn their heads to follow the movement of the Sun throughout the day.

- The vanilla flavor comes from the seed pods of the vanilla orchid. It's one of the most labor-intensive crops to cultivate, as each flower must be pollinated by hand.

o Orchids are incredibly diverse, with over 25,000 species and thousands of hybrids. They come in various sizes, shapes, and colors, making them some of the most coveted flowers among collectors.

o Some flowers open and close their petals at specific times of the day, acting like natural "clocks." The morning glory is one such flower that blooms in the morning and closes in the afternoon.

o Many perfumes and fragrances are derived from essential oils extracted from flowers. Roses, jasmine, and lavender are popular choices for creating exquisite scents.

o Some flowers are capable of self-pollination, meaning they can fertilize themselves without external assistance from pollinators like bees or butterflies.

o Although roses come in a variety of colors, blue roses don't occur naturally. Scientists have worked on creating blue roses through genetic modification.

o Some flowers, like the night-blooming cereus and moonflower, bloom only at night to attract nighttime pollinators like moths and bats.

o Cherry blossoms are celebrated in many cultures, particularly in Japan, where "hanami" festivals mark the blooming of cherry trees. These festivals often include picnics and cultural performances.

o Flowers have played roles in art and mythology throughout history. The lotus flower, for example, is a symbol of purity and enlightenment in various cultures.

o A flower's life cycle typically involves stages like germination, growth, flowering, pollination, and seed production. This cycle ensures the continuation of the plant species.

o Some flowers are used as natural insecticides. For example, the pyrethrum daisy is commonly used as a green pest control measure.

o Did you know that in Holland tulips were at one time worth more than gold?

o Some flowers are carnivorous and trap insects to digest them.

o Ever noticed why your flowers seem to lean in a certain direction? That's because they follow the path of the sun from east to west.

FRUITS AND VEGETABLES

o Kiwifruits were originally known as "Chinese gooseberries" and were first grown in China before being cultivated in New Zealand.

o Coconut water is a natural electrolyte-rich drink, making it a popular choice for rehydration.

o Grapes have been cultivated for thousands of years and are one of the oldest cultivated fruits, dating back to ancient civilizations like the Egyptians and Greeks.

o The jackfruit is the largest fruit that grows on trees, capable of reaching up to 80 pounds in weight.

o Although often treated as vegetables in cooking, tomatoes are botanically classified as fruits because they develop from the ovary of a flower and contain seeds.

o While bananas might not look like berries, they are classified as such because they have seeds on the inside and develop from a single ovary.

o Seedless watermelons are not entirely seedless. They have small, edible, and undeveloped white seeds.

o Despite their name, strawberries are not true berries. The tiny seeds on the surface are actually the fruits, while the flesh is the enlarged receptacle.

o Pineapples grow from the center of a plant, with the leaves tightly spiraling around a central core.

o The avocado is classified as a berry, and it's one of the few fruits that don't ripen on the tree. It matures after being picked.

- There are thousands of apple varieties around the world, each with its unique flavor, texture, and color.

- The durian fruit is infamous for its strong odor, often described as a mix of rotten onions, turpentine, and raw sewage. Despite the smell, it's considered a delicacy in some parts of Asia.

- Blueberries are rich in antioxidants, which help protect cells from damage and support overall health.

- The first cultivated carrots were purple, not orange. The orange carrot we know today was developed through selective breeding.

- While often claimed to be a "negative calorie" food, celery does have calories. However, it's very low in calories and can be a healthy snack option.

- Green, red, orange, and yellow bell peppers are all the same type of pepper at different stages of ripeness.

- Potatoes were first cultivated in the Andes mountains of South America over 7,000 years ago. They spread to Europe and other parts of the world over time.

- Broccoli, cauliflower, cabbage, and Brussels sprouts are all part of the same family—the cruciferous or brassica family.

- Cucumbers are made up of about 95% water, making them a hydrating and refreshing snack.

- Onions release a volatile compound when cut that reacts with the moisture in your eyes, causing tears.

- Sweet potatoes and yams are often confused, but they are distinct plants with different nutritional profiles.

o Like avocados, zucchinis are considered botanical berries, even though they're typically treated as vegetables in cooking.

o While spinach is healthy and nutrient-rich, the myth about it having exceptionally high iron content was the result of a misplaced decimal point in an early study.

o Radishes come in various colors, including red, white, purple, and black. They can also be found in unique shapes and sizes.

o The edible part of the artichoke plant is the immature flower bud. If left to mature, the bud would bloom into a vibrant blue-purple flower.

o While white cauliflower is most common, there are also orange, green, and purple varieties that offer different flavors and nutrients.

o Beets contain natural pigments that have been historically used to dye fabrics and even create natural food coloring.

HERBS AND SPICES

- Cinnamon is obtained from the inner bark of trees. It has been used for centuries for its distinct sweet and warm flavor.

- Peppermint not only adds a refreshing taste but also has a cooling sensation due to its natural compounds, like menthol.

- Saffron is one of the most expensive spices in the world because it requires a large number of delicate saffron crocus flowers to produce a small amount of the spice.

- Basil comes in different varieties, including sweet basil, Thai basil, and lemon basil, each with its unique flavor profile.

- The bright yellow color of turmeric is due to a compound called curcumin, which also has potential health benefits.

- Rosemary's needle-like leaves are highly aromatic and are often used to add a fragrant flavor to dishes.

- Coriander seeds and cilantro leaves both come from the same plant. The seeds are used as a spice, while the leaves are used as an herb.

- Cardamom pods contain small seeds with a sweet and spicy flavor, making them versatile for both sweet and savory dishes.

- Ginger adds a zesty and warming flavor to dishes. It's also used for its potential digestive and anti-inflammatory benefits.

- The Scoville Scale measures the heat of chili peppers. The Carolina Reaper holds the record as one of the spiciest peppers in the world.

o Cilantro's flavor is polarizing; some people find it refreshing, while others detect a soapy taste due to genetic differences in taste receptors.

o Kale is often referred to as a superfood due to its high nutrient content, including vitamins, minerals, and antioxidants.

o Lavender's fragrant flowers are used not only in perfumes and cosmetics but also in culinary creations like lavender-infused desserts.

o Trees share information through a "Wood Wide Web" – a network of fungi and roots. They exchange nutrients, alerts about threats, and resources. This communication system helps trees support each other.

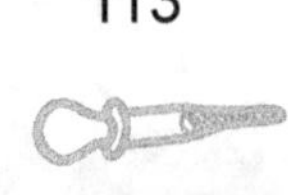

ART

ART AND ARTIST

- Picasso believed that art is done to wash away the dust of our daily lives from our souls. To briefly explain this quote, Picasso believed that art is fundamental for our souls and that it constantly craves for it. While food is eaten to replenish our body, art is used to feed the demands of the soul. Art renews and gives us happiness. How's that for artfacts?

- The oldest known cave paintings in the world date back to around 64,000 years ago. They were discovered in Altamira, Spain, and depict animals such as bison, deer, and horses.

- The art form of origami, the Japanese art of paper folding, has been around for over 1,000 years. It is believed that origami was first used for ceremonial purposes in Japan.

- The technique of collage, combining various materials to create art, was popularized by Pablo Picasso and Georges Braque during the Cubist movement.

- The ancient Egyptians used hieroglyphics to communicate through art. These intricate symbols conveyed everything from stories to religious beliefs, offering a glimpse into their civilization.

- In the modern era, artificial intelligence (AI) is being used to create art. Algorithms can generate paintings, music, and even poetry, blurring the line between human and machine creativity.

- Besides his famous paintings, Leonardo da Vinci was also an inventor! He sketched out ideas for flying machines, diving suits, and even a bicycle-like contraption.

o Some artists, known as synesthetes, experience the blending of senses. For example, they might see colors while listening to music. Kandinsky was one such artist who aimed to capture music's essence in his paintings.

o Mosaics involve arranging small pieces of material like glass, stone, or tiles to create intricate designs. Ancient Roman mosaics adorned floors and walls, depicting scenes from mythology and daily life.

o Trash artists take discarded materials like old toys, bottle caps, and cardboard to make amazing sculptures and art installations that send an eco-friendly message.

o Skywriters are like artists with airplanes! They create massive words and pictures in the sky using the smoke trails from their planes.

o Some artists create art that's invisible to the naked eye. They use ultraviolet lights to reveal hidden messages and drawings in unexpected places.

o Fire painters use controlled flames to scorch patterns onto wood and paper. The result is a mesmerizing blend of art and fire dancing together.

o Some artists use sand to create jaw-dropping images on light tables. They use their hands to shape and sculpt the sand, bringing stories to life.

o Some museums have artworks that seem to follow you with their eyes! These are called "hollow portraits," and they're optical illusions that make the subjects appear alive.

o Vincent van Gogh, known for his
breathtaking "Starry Night" painting, once said, "I often
think that the night is more alive and more richly colored
than the day." He captured the magic of the night sky with
swirling stars and vivid colors.

o Wassily Kandinsky believed that colors and shapes could
evoke emotions in the same way that
music does. He painted abstract works that aimed to convey
feelings without depicting recognizable objects.

o A lot of great artists have also had strange pets. Surrealist
painter Salvador Dalí had an anteater, which he took on a walk
through Paris. Mexican artist Frida Kahlo had more than just
one pet – she owned chickens, sparrows, macaws and
parakeets, Bonito the parrot, a fawn named Granizo, spider
monkeys Fulang Chang and Caimito de Guayabal, an eagle
called Gertrudis and hairless Xoloitzcuintli! A lot of these

o In the top 25 of the most expensive paintings, 5 of them
are by Picasso.
Do you ever wonder who is the best painter? Or do you ever
think if money really talks in the case of art? Well, in most
cases, it doesn't but it's for sure that painters like Picasso,
Pallock and Van Gogh dominate the top 25 most expensive
paintings in the world.

o Have you ever thought to yourself whether you are a math
person or humanitarian? Well, studies have shown that if you
are good at art then there is a high possibility of you being
good at math or any other technical sciences. Researchers
find that art correlates strongly with high achievements in
reading and math. How cool is that!

MUSIC

- Wolfgang Amadeus Mozart, one of the greatest composers, began composing music when he was just five years old. By the time he was a teenager, he had already composed symphonies, operas, and sonatas!

- Ludwig van Beethoven continued to compose even after he lost his hearing. His famous Ninth Symphony, which includes the "Ode to Joy," was composed when he was almost completely deaf.

- Cows definitely like classical music. Cows may produce more milk when they are listening to classical music!

- Turn up the volume! If you want more milk, play more classical.

- The first portable music players were called "walkman." They allowed people to carry their favorite music with them wherever they went, and they were quite popular before the age of smartphones.

- Some scientists believe that plants can respond to music. In an experiment, plants exposed to classical music grew faster and healthier compared to those without music.

- Beatboxing is a form of vocal percussion where artists create rhythms and sounds using only their mouths. Some beatboxers can mimic the sounds of drums, instruments, and even record scratching!

- Music therapy is used to help people recover from illnesses and manage stress. Listening to or creating music can have a positive impact on our mental and emotional well-being.

- Some songbirds, like canaries, learn to sing from other birds around them. They're like the musicians who learn by listening and practicing, just like humans!

- Different cultures use drums to communicate across long distances. African "talking drums" can mimic the tones and rhythms of speech, allowing messages to be relayed far and wide

- Some animals have a natural sense of rhythm and melody. For example, certain birds like the lyrebird can mimic a wide range of sounds, including chainsaws and camera shutters, creating their own unique tunes.

- The quietest place on Earth is an anechoic chamber, designed to absorb all sound. It's so quiet that you can hear your own heartbeat and even the sound of your internal organs working!

- Musicians use math without even realizing it! The relationships between musical notes are based on mathematical ratios, creating harmony and melodies that sound pleasing to our ears.

- Autotune is a technology used in music production to correct pitch. It can make even the most out-of-tune notes sound perfect, but it's also used creatively to create unique vocal effects.

- Melodies from Space: The Voyager 1 spacecraft, launched in 1977, carries a golden record with sounds and music from Earth. It's like a musical message in a bottle sent out into the cosmos.

- Listening to music can evoke powerful memories and emotions. It's like a time machine that takes us back to specific moments in our lives.

o   Most orchestras consist of musical instruments, like trumpets, flutes, etc. But not this orchestra! An orchestra in Australia plays music…But the musical instruments are made from veggies! That's right: an orchestra that has carrots, potatoes, and others. Weird!

o   Music Helps Plants Grow Faster. According to a study by scientists from South Korea, plants grow at a faster pace when they are played classical music. Using 14 different pieces of music, the scientists played music to a rice field and studied the results. Findings were that the music helped the crops grow and even suggested evidence that plants could "hear". We suggest practicing your instrument in your veggie garden!

o   Studying music is an actual workout for your brain. Learning an instrument has been proven to help students in myriad ways from mastery of memorisation, pattern recognition and emotional development. Students who have experience with music performance or taking music appreciation courses score higher on the SAT(Scholastic Aptitude Test). A report indicated that they score, on average, 63 points higher on verbal and 44 points higher on math. You can start your musical journey with us!

MUSICAL INSTRUMENTS

o The Didgeridoo's Unique Sound: The didgeridoo, an instrument from Australia, is made from a hollowed-out tree trunk or branch. Its distinctive sound comes from a technique called "circular breathing," where the player inhales through their nose while blowing air out of their mouth, allowing continuous sound.

o The harp is often associated with angels and heavenly music. It's played by plucking its strings, producing enchanting and magical sounds.

o The electric guitar changed the world of music forever. Les Paul, a pioneer in electric guitar design, was also an inventor. He created the first solid-body electric guitar and helped shape rock 'n' roll history.

o Fire organs are instruments that use controlled flames to create sound. The flames "dance" to the music's vibrations, producing a mesmerizing visual and auditory experience.

o The flute is one of the oldest musical instruments known to humans. Flutes made from animal bones have been found in ancient archaeological sites, dating back tens of thousands of years.

o The glass harmonica, invented by Benjamin Franklin, produces ethereal and haunting sounds by rubbing moistened fingers along the edges of rotating glass bowls. It's said to have an otherworldly quality that can even mesmerize listeners.

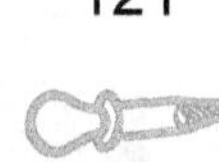

o   The theremin is one of the few instruments that doesn't require physical contact to play. Skilled theremin players can create complex melodies, and some even use their bodies to manipulate the electromagnetic fields for intricate compositions.

o   Astounding Alphorn: The alphorn is a long wooden horn traditionally used in the Swiss Alps. Its deep, resonant tones can carry for miles and were originally used to communicate between mountain villages.

o   Filling glasses with different amounts of water produces a variety of pitches. By carefully tapping the glasses with a spoon, musicians can play melodies with this unexpected and creative "glassophone."

o   Sonic Boom of the Whip: The whip, usually associated with cowboy culture, can also be used as a musical instrument. Skilled whip-crackers can produce a loud, cracking sound that resembles a sonic boom, creating a rhythmic percussion element.

o   Musical tesla coils are electrifying instruments that use electricity to create music. As electric discharges jump between coils, they produce audible tones that can be manipulated to play melodies.

o   Intricate Hurdy-Gurdy: The hurdy-gurdy is a unique instrument that combines elements of strings and keys. Players crank a wheel, causing strings to vibrate while pressing keys to create different pitches, resulting in a distinctive medieval sound.

- Whirling Bullhorn: The bullhorn, or vuvuzela, is a horn-shaped instrument known for its loud and resonant sound. It gained global attention during the 2010 World Cup, where thousands of fans created a symphony of buzzing tones.

THE MOVIES

- The first cinemas were opened in the early 1900s. Before then, films were shown in public halls, theaters or at funfairs!

- Movies used to be recorded on film and were then shown to audiences by being run through a projector on reels. Nowadays, the process is all digital, with smaller cameras and digital projectors in cinemas.

- Films were originally made without sound. Known now as 'silent movies,' when they were shown there was often a live piano player, organist or small group of musicians present to add atmosphere.

- The first public movie screening took place in 1895 by the Lumière brothers. The audience was astounded when they saw a train approaching on the screen and thought it was actually coming towards them!

- Many movie scenes set in spectacular locations were actually filmed in front of green screens. The magic of visual effects transforms these simple backgrounds into breathtaking landscapes.

- During the era of silent films, pranks on set were common. Charlie Chaplin once replaced a drink with gasoline in a scene, causing his co-star to spit out a mouthful in shock!

- Movie sound effects are often created in a studio using everyday items. The sound of walking on gravel might be made by walking on cornflakes, and the squelching sound of mud might come from plunging hands into jelly!

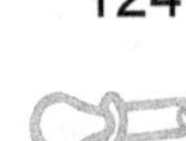

o Voice actors bring animated characters to life through their expressive performances. Sometimes, they even act out their scenes to capture the character's emotions and movements.

o Movies often use camera tricks to create illusions. Techniques like forced perspective make objects appear larger or smaller than they actually are, adding an element of surprise to the scene.

o Movie scores and soundtracks play a crucial role in shaping the emotional impact of scenes. Subtle melodies can intensify suspense or uplift moments of triumph, weaving a powerful auditory tapestry.

o Actors often learn new accents or dialects for their roles. Mastering a different way of speaking adds authenticity and depth to their characters.

o Lighting designers shape the mood and atmosphere of a film with their artistry. Subtle shifts in lighting can change the tone of a scene from ordinary to extraordinary.

o Advances in technology have given rise to mind-bending visual effects that seamlessly blend the real and the digital. From shrinking superheroes to intergalactic battles, the possibilities are limitless.

o Some cities have dedicated museums and exhibits that celebrate the art of filmmaking, offering visitors a behind-the-scenes look at iconic props, costumes, and sets.

ACTORS AND ACTRESS

o Some actors use real emotions and experiences to enhance their performances. Drawing from personal stories can make scenes more authentic and moving for both the actors and the audience.

o Dedicated actors immerse themselves in their roles, sometimes undergoing incredible physical transformations. They gain or lose weight, change hairstyles, and even alter their appearance to authentically portray characters.

o Makeup artists and visual effects experts work their magic to age actors for specific roles, allowing performers to convincingly portray characters spanning decades.

o Some actors are fluent in multiple languages, allowing them to take on roles from around the world and connect with audiences globally.

o Actors undergo rigorous physical training to prepare for roles, whether it's bulking up, learning martial arts, or developing dance skills for musicals.

o Some actors possess unexpected talents, like musical skills, painting, or even stand-up comedy, showcasing their versatility beyond the world of acting.

o Great actors tap into their empathy to understand and embody characters' emotions, allowing them to connect deeply with both the roles and the audience.

o Did you know that some actors have directed movies they starred in? Imagine the challenge of not only bringing a character to life but also guiding the entire film's creative vision.

o Before fame, some actors pursued entirely different careers. Harrison Ford worked as a carpenter, and Christopher Lee served in the British Special Forces during World War II.

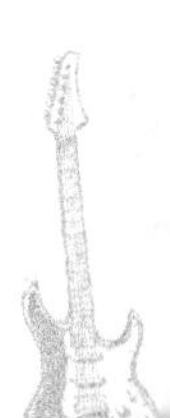

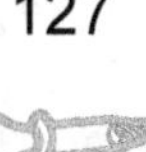

SPORTS

SPORTSPEOPLE

- Michael Jordan, one of basketball's greatest players, once held a record for the longest dunk from the free-throw line, soaring through the air to make an unbelievable shot.

- Soccer star Ronaldinho isn't just known for his skills on the field – he's also a master juggler, often seen juggling a soccer ball with his feet, head, and even shoulders!

- Table tennis champion Jan-Ove Waldner is so skilled that he's known as the "Mozart of Table Tennis." His precise shots and strategic moves leave opponents amazed.

- Natalia Molchanova, a freediving world champion, held an incredible record of diving down to 101 meters on a single breath, showcasing the power of mind and body control.

- Lolo Jones is not only an Olympic hurdler but also a bobsledder! She transitioned from track and field to bobsleigh and competed in both the Summer and Winter Olympics.

- Sky Brown became the youngest female skateboarder to compete in the Olympics at just 13 years old, showing the world that age is no barrier to pursuing your passions.

- Vince Carter's legendary dunks in basketball earned him the nickname "Half Man, Half Amazing." His ability to soar above the rim captivated fans worldwide.

- Dean Karnazes ran 50 marathons in 50 states in 50 consecutive days – an incredible feat of endurance that showcases the limitless potential of the human body.

o Alex Honnold achieved fame for free solo climbing El Capitan, a 3,000-foot vertical rock face, without any ropes or safety equipment – a jaw-dropping display of courage.

o Tony Hawk landed the first documented "900" – two and a half spins on a skateboard in mid-air – a move that pushed the boundaries of what was considered possible.

o Michael Jordan holds the record for the most consecutive games played with at least 10 points scored - the record is 866.

o Danica Patrick shattered gender norms by becoming one of the most successful female race car drivers, competing in the male-dominated world of motorsports.

o Michael Phelps holds the record for the most Olympic medals won. The US swimmer Michael Phelps won a total of 23 Olympics medals, including 23 Gold medals. He competed in four Olympics Games between the years 2004 to 2016.

o The longest recorded tennis match lasted for 11 hours. This took place at Wimbledon in 2010. John Isner won this match against Nicolas Mahut and it took over 3 days to complete.

o Only two athletes have won gold medals at both the Summer and Winter Olympics. Sweden's Gillis Grafstrom won the gold in figure skating at the 1920 Summer Olympics and again in 1924 and 1928 when it moved to the Winter Games. American athlete, Eddie Eagan, won gold in boxing in 1920 and again in the team bobsled event at the 1932 Winter Games.

SPORTS

- Baseball is often called America's pastime, but its origins can be traced back to a game called "rounders," played in England in the 18th century.

- The fastest 100m running backward was completed in just 13.6 seconds. It's an impressive skill that requires a unique set of muscles and coordination!

- Chess boxing is a hybrid sport where competitors alternate between playing chess and boxing rounds. It combines mental strategy and physical endurance.

- Parkour athletes, known as traceurs, use acrobatics and agility to navigate urban environments. It's like turning the whole city into an obstacle course.

- Unicycle hockey is played on unicycles, combining hockey skills with the challenge of staying balanced on one wheel.

- Octopush, also known as underwater hockey, is played at the bottom of a swimming pool. Players use a stick to push a puck into the opposing team's goal.

- Just like in regular rugby, underwater rugby players try to score goals by placing a ball in the opponent's goal. The twist? It's all done underwater.

- Chess boxing is a hybrid sport where competitors alternate between playing chess and boxing rounds. It combines mental strategy and physical endurance.

- Believe it or not, extreme ironing is a real sport where participants iron clothes in challenging and remote locations, like on top of a mountain or underwater.

o   Golf is one of only two sports every played on the moon. In 1971, Alan Shepard hit a ball with a six-iron while on the moon as part of the Apollo 14 mission. The other sport was a javelin toss, during the same visit.

o   Mountain unicycling, or MUni, involves riding unicycles on rugged mountain trails. It requires impressive balance and control.

o   In speed climbing, athletes race to reach the top of a climbing wall in the shortest time possible. It's one of the disciplines in sport climbing.

o   Roller derby is a fast-paced contact sport played on roller skates. Teams race around an oval track while trying to score points by passing opponents.

o   Just like arm wrestling, toe wrestling involves competitors trying to pin each other's toes to the ground.

o   Just like arm wrestling, toe wrestling involves competitors trying to pin each other's toes to the ground.

o   An egg and spoon race is a classic children's game where participants balance an egg on a spoon and race to the finish line without dropping it.

o   Ferret legging is a bizarre sport where participants place live ferrets in their pants and see how long they can endure their bites and scratches.

o   Shin kicking is a traditional English sport where competitors stuff their pants with straw and kick each other's shins until one gives up.

o   Unicycle hockey is played on unicycles, combining hockey skills with the challenge of staying balanced on one wheel.

GAMES AND PASTIMES

- Dice games have been played for thousands of years. In ancient times, dice were made from various materials, including bones, wood, and even fruit pits.

- Jousting, a popular medieval sport, pitted knights against each other in mounted combat. They aimed to unseat their opponent or break their lance – a thrilling spectacle!

- Origami, the art of paper folding, originated in Japan. Mastering intricate folds, enthusiasts create beautiful figures and objects without any cutting or gluing.

- The ancient Egyptian game "Senet" wasn't just for fun; it was thought to represent the journey of the soul to the afterlife. Winning meant a successful passage to the divine realm.

- The Rubik's Cube, invented by Ernő Rubik, became a global sensation in the 1980s. With billions of possible combinations, solving it requires patience and clever twists.

- Kites were invented in China over 2,000 years ago. They were initially used for military signaling, but they soon became a favorite pastime around the world.

- The first crossword puzzle was created by Arthur Wynne and published in the New York World in 1913. The initial reaction was lukewarm, but the concept grew into a worldwide phenomenon.

- The art of creating intricate mandalas, originating in various cultures, has therapeutic benefits. The act of coloring or crafting these patterns can promote relaxation and focus.

- Ice skating, whether on a frozen pond or in a rink, offers a graceful way to glide and spin. It's a joyful winter activity enjoyed by people of all ages.

- The ancient Chinese game of Go is known for its profound complexity, with more possible moves on the board than there are atoms in the observable universe.

- The Rubik's Cube, invented in 1974 by Ernő Rubik, has over 43 quintillion possible combinations, making it a challenging puzzle loved by millions worldwide.

- Chess grandmaster Paul Morphy, in the 19th century, could play up to eight simultaneous games blindfolded, keeping track of all the moves in his mind.

- Record-Setting Card Tower: The tallest house of cards ever built had 25 stories and was constructed using over 6,000 cards.

- An extreme version of Rock-Paper-Scissors involves skydiving participants playing the game mid-air before deploying their parachutes.

- Speedcubing involves solving a Rubik's Cube as quickly as possible. The current world record for solving a 3x3 cube is under 4 seconds.